CW00730412

The Macedonian Army of Philip II and Alexander the Great, 359–323 BC

The Macedonian Army of Philip II and Alexander the Great, 359–323 BC

History, organization and equipment

Gabriele Esposito

Pen & Sword
MILITARY

First published in Great Britain in 2022
by Pen & Sword Military
An imprint of Pen & Sword Books Limited
47 Church Street
Barnsley
South Yorkshire
S70 2AS

ISBN 978 1 52678 735 4

A CIP catalogue record for this book is
available from the British Library

Typeset in Adobe Caslon
by Mac Style

Printed and bound in India by Replika Press Pvt. Ltd.

Pen & Sword Books Limited incorporates the imprints of Atlas,
Archaeology, Aviation, Discovery, Family History, Fiction, History, Maritime,
Military, Military Classics, Politics, Select, Transport, True Crime, Air World,
Frontline Publishing, Leo Cooper, Remember When, Seaforth Publishing,
The Praetorian Press, Wharncliffe Local History, Wharncliffe Transport,
Wharncliffe True Crime and White Owl.

For a complete list of Pen & Sword titles please contact
PEN & SWORD BOOKS LIMITED
47 Church Street, Barnsley, South Yorkshire, S70 2AS, England
E-mail: enquiries@pen-and-sword.co.uk
Website: www. pen-and-sword.co.uk

Contents

Gabriele Esposito is a military historian who works as a freelance author and researcher for some of the most important publishing houses in the military history sector. In particular, he is an expert specializing in uniformology: his interests and expertise range from the ancient civilizations to modern post-colonial conflicts. During recent years, he has conducted and published several researches on the military history of the Latin American countries, with special attention on the War of the Triple Alliance and the War of the Pacific. He is among the leading experts on the military history of the Italian Wars of Unification and the Spanish Carlist Wars. His books and essays are published on a regular basis by Osprey Publishing, Winged Hussar Publishing and Libreria Editrice Goriziana; he is also the author of numerous military history articles appearing in specialized magazines like *Ancient Warfare Magazine*, *Medieval Warfare Magazine*, *The Armourer*, *History of War*, *Guerres et Histoire*, *Focus Storia* and *Focus Storia Wars*.

Acknowledgements

This book is dedicated to my beloved parents, Maria Rosaria and Benedetto, for their immense love and great support in every phase of my life. Thanks to their precious advice, the present publication is a much better product: their great intelligence is always a secure guide for me. A very special mention goes to the German re-enactment group and living history association 'Hetairoi', for providing me the magnificent and detailed photographs that illustrate this book. In particular, I want to express my deep gratitude to Thorsten Schillo: he enjoyed and supported the idea of this book from the beginnings and has helped me in every phase of its production with great generosity. I want to express my gratitude also to the other two groups that collaborated with me for this title: 'Athenea Prómakhos' from Spain, in the person of Jonatan Prieto, and 'Ancient Thrace' from Bulgaria, in the person of Petar Chapkanov. Without their incredible work of research and re-enactment, the present work would have not been the same. A very special thanks goes to Philip Sidnell, the commissioning editor of my books for Pen & Sword: his love for history and his passion for publishing are the key factors behind the success of our publications. Last but not least, a special mention goes to the production manager of this title, Matt Jones, for his great competence and patience, and many thanks also to Tony Walton for his usual incredible work on my manuscripts.

Introduction

The main aim of this book is to present a detailed analysis of the organization, combat experiences, tactics and equipment of Alexander the Great's Macedonian Army. Alexander's army is one of the most famous military forces of Antiquity, well known because of its most important component: the iconic heavy infantry phalanx, a tactical formation that gave victory to Alexander in several pitched battles. To understand the reasons behind the great conqueror's military successes, we will follow the history of the Kingdom of Macedonia since its first significant political experiences up to the rise of Philip II, Alexander's brilliant father and one of the greatest military reformers of the ancient world. We will see how the Macedonians played an important role in the history of Greece before the ascendancy of Philip, and will examine how the latter was able to subdue most of the southern Balkans in just a few years. A lot of space will be devoted to the military reforms carried out by Alexander's father, in order to describe the structure and organization of Macedonia's most iconic military units: the foot companions, the horse companions and the hypaspists. The book will then provide an analysis of Alexander's early military campaigns and of his subsequent great victories in Asia: at the River Granicus, Issus, Tyre, Gaza, Gaugamela, the Persian Gate, Sogdian Rock and River Hydaspes. By describing the various campaigns and battles, we will also follow the internal evolution of the Macedonian Army, with an analysis of its lesser-known troop types such as the light infantry/cavalry and the allied/mercenary forces provided by the Greeks. The tactics employed by Alexander's soldiers will be explained in great detail across the whole text, and there will be a final chapter entirely devoted to a description of the panoply used by the various components of the Macedonian Army, from the long pikes of the phalangites to the light javelins of the tribal peltasts.

Chapter 1

Macedonia before Philip II

For a very long time, the Kingdom of Macedonia was not considered as part of the Greek world because it was located on the northern edge of the Hellenic kingdoms and its inhabitants were quite different from those of the great Greek urban centres like Athens or Sparta. Although the Macedonians spoke Greek and practised the same religion as the southern Greeks, they had a completely different lifestyle. Primarily, they did not live in large cities like the rest of the Greeks, their settlements instead being dispersed across a vast countryside and consisting of small rural villages. In addition, the Macedonian economy and society were completely different from those of the other Greeks: commerce and craftsmanship were quite underdeveloped in Macedonia, with the local economy instead based on agriculture and horse breeding. Agriculture was the main occupation of the Macedonians, the majority of whom were free men who owned a small farm, sustaining their families with the products of their land and having large flocks of sheep or goats. The breeding of horses was particularly important for the economy of Macedonia, since these animals were used in war and could also be sold to the southern Greeks in exchange for significant sums of money. Macedonian society retained a very tribal nature for a long time, with the development of a centralized state being extremely slow. Each village was dominated by its own noble warlord, who was at the head of a personal retinue of warriors. No form of democracy existed and the king exerted only nominal power over the state's many nobles. These nobles, with their warriors, fought as horsemen and were extremely warlike: pillaging and raiding were common activities. The most important cities of Greece were characterized by the presence of a strong middle class, whose members made up the bulk of the armies assembled by the various urban centres. Indeed, it was from these merchants and craftsmen that the heavy infantry of the hoplites were recruited. Macedonia had very few slaves; all the subjects of the king were free men, but between them and the aristocracy there was no middle class. Macedonian armies mostly consisted of cavalry, which comprised the nobles and their personal retinues; the great majority of the population was excluded from military life, which meant the kingdom was quite weak from a military point of view. Neither could the Macedonians be compared with the other Greeks from a cultural point of view: they spoke Greek with a very distinctive 'rural' accent and

Philip II of Macedonia, father of Alexander the Great and reformer of the Macedonian Army. The warrior king was wounded several times during his life and even lost an eye. (*Photo and copyright by Hetairoi*)

Philip II in his parade armour made of iron, which was decorated with bronze attachments. (*Photo and copyright by Hetairoi*)

did not practise philosophy like the Athenians. Macedonian civilization was thus a simplified version of the Greek culture, to the point that the Greeks considered the Macedonians to be semi-barbarians who had very little in common with them. This was partly true, the Kingdom of Macedonia being located in the heart of the Balkans and thus heavily influenced by several different civilizations.

At this point, it is important to have a clear idea of which populations lived around the Macedonians and how they interacted with the Kingdom of Macedonia. To the north of Macedon were the Paeonians, a people of mixed Thraco-Illyrian descent living on the border between two worlds: the Thracian in the east and the Illyrian in the west. The Paeonians were extremely warlike, and were considered by the Greeks as the most ferocious warriors of the Balkans. They spent most of their life fighting between themselves and against the nearby tribes of the Thracians/Illyrians. Their society had a tribal organization and they all fought as excellent light infantrymen. Living on a harsh territory that was mostly covered with mountains, they had learned how to survive during cold months with very few resources and could endure any sacrifice in case of war. Pillaging was one of their most important activities, and most of their bloody raids were usually directed against Macedonia. Both the Greeks and the Macedonians feared the Paeonian warriors, who were considered extremely wild and showed very little respect for any of the social/religious practices of the Hellenic world. The Paeonians consisted of several different tribes, having their own warlords and establishing their own alliances with the Thracian and Illyrian communities living on their borders. The most important Paeonian tribe was that of the Agrianes, who were under a strong Thracian influence from a military point of view and were deadly warriors equipped with javelins.

To the west of Macedonia was the land inhabited by the Illyrians, who controlled a large portion of the western Balkans corresponding to the territories of the former Yugoslavia (from modern Slovenia in the north to the central areas of Albania in the south). The Illyrians were divided into several different tribes and were ruled by numerous warlords; sometimes one of these could become stronger than the others and assume the title of 'king', but they only had a nominal importance. Broadly speaking, the Illyrian tribes living in the north were not influenced by Greek civilization, whereas those in the south were seen as more 'civilized' according to contemporary Greek standards. Illyria also comprised a large portion of coastline, from which the Illyrians were able to control most of the Adriatic Sea until the naval ascendancy of Rome. Over time, they became infamous as pirates and started to conduct frequent raids across the Adriatic. Like the Paeonians, the Illyrians also lived in small villages and their society was a rural one, and they too launched frequent incursions against Macedonia.

To the east of Macedonia lived the Thracians, one of the most important peoples of Antiquity. They were divided into more than forty tribes, which were constantly at war with each other: Thracian society was an extremely warlike one, in which warfare was considered one of the most important and most normal elements in a man's life. From an economic point of view, the Thracians practised breeding much more than agriculture: the great majority of them, in fact, were shepherds and lived from the products obtained from their sheep and goats. Inter-tribal skirmishes and raids were usually sparked by controversies starting among shepherds for control of the pastures. The majority of the Thracians did not live in permanent settlements, because they followed their herds during most of the year. Consequently, until the arrival of the first Greek colonists, Thrace did not have any major city. Raiding the village of a rival tribe was a normal occurrence for a semi-nomad Thracian community, since skirmishes and minor 'local' wars were seen as a great occasion to enlarge herds by capturing sheep or goats from their enemy. This kind of warfare was common to all the Balkan peoples, including the Macedonians. The territory of Thrace (present-day Bulgaria), mostly covered by hills, was not well suited to armies equipped with heavy armour and moving in close formations. Indeed, the only way to move rapidly and fight effectively in the Thracian hinterland was to act as skirmishers, equipped with throwing weapons and trained in light infantry tactics. The territory of Thrace, however, also comprised some plains where the local communities bred excellent horses. The Thracian tribes were distinguished between those of the mountains and those of the plains, according to the morphology of the hills or valleys on which they lived.

According to ancient authors such as Herodotus, the Thracians were the most numerous people of Europe: if united into a single kingdom, they could have defeated and conquered all the ancient nations living along their borders. Fortunately for the latter, however, the Thracians always preferred inter-tribal warfare to invasions directed against foreign peoples. In Thrace, the profession of warrior was highly honoured, and was considered superior to all others. Showing courage in battle was fundamental for a Thracian man to acquire a respected personal reputation. Generally speaking, however, Thracian warriors were not famous for their martial discipline: they loved plunder more than anything else, and this frequently caused them serious problems during a battle or campaign. The Thracians never lost their original character of semi-nomadic raiders, even after centuries of close contact with the major civilizations of the Mediterranean. Nothing was more important for them than personal wealth, and every possible method to augment that wealth was considered legitimate. Like the Paeonians and the Illyrians, the Thracians organized frequent raids against the rural communities of Macedon, in particular invading

Macedonian phalangite with leather muscle cuirass. (*Photo and copyright by Hetairoi*)

Macedonian phalangite, with pelte round shield and bronze greaves. (*Photo and copyright by Hetairoi*)

the eastern portion of the Kingdom of Macedonia on several occasions. When a large part of the Thracian tribes was finally unified into a single state, known as the Odrysian Kingdom, they became a very serious threat to the internal stability of Macedonia due to their impressive military resources and to expansionist ambitions.

As is clear from the above description of their neighbours, the Macedonians can be considered to be one of the most 'unlucky' peoples of Antiquity: they were surrounded by numerous warlike communities and were too weak militarily to put up an effective resistance against raids or invasions by these 'barbarians' along their borders.

South-west of Macedonia was the partly Hellenized Kingdom of Epirus, whose inhabitants had a lot in common with the Macedonians: they spoke Greek and believed in the same gods as the Greeks, but were also considered 'barbarians' by the Greeks since they had a society organized along tribal lines and a lower level of civilization that was largely a rural one. Epirus, roughly corresponding to present-day central and southern Albania, was under strong influence from the Illyrian tribes living on its northern borders and was only a marginal player in the Greek political games. Traditionally, it had always been inhabited by three main tribes: the Chaonians in the north, the Molossians in the centre and the Thesprotians in the south. Until 370 BC, these three tribes were not organized into a single state and were frequently at war with each other. Differently from Greece, Epirus had no cities, with all the Epirotes living in small villages dispersed across the countryside. Originally, the three tribes of Epirus had been nomadic groups and thus had been constantly at war against the Illyrians raiding from the north. This political situation continued until 370 BC, when the Molossians started to expand at the expense of the other two tribal groups. After several years of internal wars, the Molossians were finally able to unify Epirus and form a centralized kingdom, ruled by the royal family of the Aecides. Epirus and Macedonia had an enemy in common: Illyria. As a result, they started to collaborate in order to limit the expansionist ambitions of the Illyrians.

To the south-east of Macedonia were the Greek cities of the Chalcidian Peninsula and the fertile region of Thessaly. With the end of the so-called Dark Ages, the population of mainland Greece started to grow at an impressive rate and all the newly founded *poleis* (independent cities or states) had to introduce measures to control the demography of their communities. Greece was still a poor country at that time and its territory was mostly covered with mountains, so the Greek cities could not practise agriculture on a large scale and were forced to resettle a substantial portion of their citizens outside the borders of mainland Greece. During the eighth and seventh centuries BC, many thousands of Greek colonists departed their mother cities in search of a new land where they could found their own *poleis*. These major migratory movements of the Greeks were directed towards the Western Mediterranean, where they created many flourishing colonies in southern Italy. However, they also settled along the coastline of southern Thrace, extending from the Chalcidian Peninsula to the Dardanelles Straits, which was the first target of the Greek colonists during their expansion eastwards. When it was realized that the hills inhabited by the Thracians were rich in precious metals like gold or silver, the Greek penetration in Thrace became more significant. The city-states of mainland Greece were in constant search of new natural resources in order to sustain the great commercial expansion of their communities. By founding new colonies in the east, they could resolve the problem of over-population while acquiring control over strategic local natural resources. To control the land to build new settlements, however, the Greeks had to fight with the local Thracian tribes, who had no intention of welcoming the foreign intruders. During their early attempts to colonize the Thracian coastline, the Greeks experienced many difficulties, with the local population being warlike and wild by comparison with Greek standards of the time. Thrace, however, was seen as a land of opportunities and the Greeks maintained their push to colonize the region. During this initial period of colonization, which lasted until the outbreak of the Persian Wars in the fifth century BC, the Greeks founded several settlements along the coastline of southern Thrace. These rich commercial outposts established by the Greeks soon transformed themselves into thriving cities, whose relations with the Thracians were often quite complicated. Nevertheless, after several decades of minor wars and frequent skirmishes, it became clear to the Thracian tribes that they could not destroy the Greek colonies. The new settlements were strongly defended by thick walls, and the Thracians were not able to conduct successful siege operations. Consequently, with the Chalcidian Peninsula now in Greek hands, Macedonia had become a landlocked country, depending entirely on foreign merchants for the importing or exporting of goods since it did not have a navy of its own.

Thessaly was one of the most atypical regions of Greece at this time, being part of the Greek world but having several peculiar features that could not be found in other areas of the Hellenic civilization. At the beginning of the Classical period, Thessaly was still only partly urbanized and was dominated by an aristocracy of local warlords who based their power on large retinues of cavalrymen. Traditionally, Thessaly had been divided into four semi-independent cantons, which recognized a sort of formal supreme authority of an elected ruler known as a '*tagos*'. This political organization could be described as a confederation: when the ruling *tagos* was strong, the cantons were kept under central control; but when the *tagos* appeared weak, each canton acted as an independent state. Civil wars were frequent. Thessaly contained many precious natural resources and was the only area of Greece where horse-breeding was practised on a large scale. According to ancient sources, the best horsemen and horses

Macedonian foot companion with Pilos helmet and linen cuirass. During marches, the long sarissa was dismantled in two parts and was carried on the shoulders. (*Photo and copyright by Hetairoi*)

Macedonian foot companion with the Vergina Star painted on the external surface of his pelte shield. This symbol, also known as the Argead Star, was distinctive of the Macedonian royal family. (*Photo and copyright by Hetairoi*)

of the Hellenic world all came from Thessaly. In addition, from a strategic point of view, the fertile and rich Thessalian plains linked mainland Greece to Macedonia and the heart of the Balkans. Being the only plain region in a country covered by mountains, Thessaly was a crucible of contrasting political interests and a target of conquest for the bordering cities and kingdoms.

Until 515 BC, the small Kingdom of Macedonia remained at the margins of the Hellenic world. Its rulers did not have stable diplomatic relations with other states and exerted only a very limited control over their aristocracy. In addition to this, the realm was under the constant threat of raids by the warlike peoples living on its borders. This situation only started to change in 513 BC, when a new military power appeared in the eastern Balkans: the mighty Persian Empire ruled by the Achaemenid dynasty. During that year, the Persian monarch Darius I conducted a military campaign in Scythia and Thrace. The Scythians, a strong nomadic people living in present-day Ukraine, had been allies of the Persians during their attack on Babylon, but had then turned into a dangerous menace for the vast empire that the Achaemenids were building. As a result, hostilities began between the Persians and Scythians. Darius, wishing to eliminate once and for all these troublesome nomads, mounted an assault against the Scythians' main European territories in southern Ukraine after crossing the Bosphorus Straits from Asia Minor (using a bridge of boats). While moving north, the Persians crossed Thrace and subdued (albeit temporarily) most of the local tribes. The Scythians used scorched-earth tactics throughout the campaign, which enabled them to retreat across the immense plains of Ukraine without fighting a single pitched battle against the Persians. Darius' expedition ended in a stalemate and the retreat of the Achaemenids to their own territories. During the campaign, however, Persian troops reached the borders of Macedonia and Achaemenid ambassadors met with the local king, Amyntas I. Impressed by the military might of the Persians, Amyntas accepted Achaemenid suzerainty over his realm by performing the 'surrender ceremony' that was usually required by the Persians when subjugating a new territory. This highly symbolic act consisted of offering 'earth and water' to the Achaemenid ambassadors as a sign of submission to the Great King of the Persian Empire. As a result, from 511 BC, Amyntas became a vassal of Darius, although his kingdom was not transformed into a Persian satrapy (province) but was permitted to retain its autonomy. After these first Achaemenid forays in the Balkans, the Scythians and Thracians returned to their previous independent condition, although the Persians started to consider those territories that they had conquered in 513–511 BC as part of their empire and thus organized an expedition to reconquer them in 492 BC. This was probably intended as a preparatory operation in view of future offensives against Greece: the Persian Army

Macedonian foot companion wearing linen cuirass reinforced with bronze scales on the sides. (*Photo and copyright by Hetairoi*)

Macedonian phalangite wearing leather boots. In this photo it is possible to appreciate the detail of the pike's butt spike (see also pages 17 and 122). (*Photo and copyright by Hetairoi*)

needed to have a base on the European continent. The Persian expeditionary corps of 492 BC was guided by Mardonius, son-in-law of Darius I, and departed from the Anatolian region of Cilicia in modern-day south-east Turkey.

The Persian Army advanced by land up to the Hellespont in northern Anatolia, marching along the coastline in order to retain direct contact with the fleet. At this point, all the troops were embarked on the ships and crossed the Hellespont without any particular problems. Once in Europe, the Persians focused on re-subjugating the Thracian tribes one by one: since the tribes were politically divided, the occupation of southern Thrace was not a difficult task for Mardonius. By now the Persians had a solid base in Europe, but instead of then moving north to fight against the Scythians, the Achaemenid forces moved west in order to enter Greece from the north. The Persians quickly reached Macedonia for a second time, and again received an act of formal submission from the local king, Alexander I. Despite formally being a loyal subject of the Persian Empire, Alexander wished to free his country from Achaemenid 'protection' and did his best to help the Greeks with supplies and advice during the ensuing Persian invasions of their territory. As a client king of the Persian Empire, Alexander I had to supply troops for its invasion of Greece during 480 and 479 BC, known as the Second Persian War. At the same time, however, he secretly informed the Greeks about the Persian Army's movements and saved them from a crushing defeat in Thessaly by suggesting an alternative military strategy. In 479 BC, after having been defeated at sea the previous year at the Battle of Salamis, the Persians were defeated on land by the Greeks at the decisive Battle of Plataea, and were subsequently forced to abandon the northern regions of Greece that they had conquered. During its retreat across northern Thessaly and Macedonia, what remained of the Persian Army was attacked by the Macedonians of Alexander I, who now changed sides to regain the independence of their realm. A pitched battle between the Macedonians and Persians took place at the estuary of the River Strymon, where 43,000 Achaemenid soldiers were crushed. Alexander I thus became one of the most important kings in the history of Macedonia, being the first to 'move' his realm into the cultural sphere of the Hellenic world. He was the first Macedonian who was permitted to participate to the Olympic Games in 504 BC, and was the first Macedonian ruler to establish a proper royal court (where the famous Greek poets Pindar and Bacchylides were active). Due to the precious help provided to the Greeks during the Second Persian War, Alexander I was even given the honorific title of 'philellene', or 'friend of the Greeks'.

After Alexander I's death in 454 BC, Macedonia experienced a series of internal difficulties. The various tribes rebelled against the central authority of the Argead dynasty, which had ruled the kingdom for more than two centuries. In addition, a violent civil war broke out between two of Alexander I's sons: Perdiccas II and Philip.

Full panoply of a Macedonian phalangite. (*Photo and copyright by Hetairoi*)

This internal conflict saw the intervention of Athens, which sent military contingents to Macedonia and supported both pretenders during different phases of the civil war. The Athenians wanted to weaken Macedonia as much as possible and to have a puppet monarch on its throne. While these events were taking place on the northern borders of Greece, the Peloponnesian War broke out between Athens and Sparta in the south. At this point, the Athenians changed their strategy in Macedonia and evacuated their troops from the region. By 430 BC, most of the Thracian tribes had been unified into a single realm, known as the Odrysian Kingdom from the name of the tribe that dominated it. This realm, ruled by the great warlord Sitalces, bordered with Macedonia along the course of the River Strymon. During the Peloponnesian War, the Odrysian Kingdom was an ally of Athens, and in 429 BC it assembled a large army of over 150,000 warriors and invaded Macedonia. After rapidly subduing Macedonia, the Thracians moved south in order to conquer the Greek cities of

Personal equipment of a Macedonian phalangite, including Thracian/Phrygian helmet. (*Photo and copyright by Hetairoi*)

the Chalcidian Peninsula that were allied to Sparta. According to plans that had been agreed with the Athenians, Sitalces' army was to have been supported by the Athenian navy during the difficult siege operations against the Chalcidian cities. When the Thracians arrived in the Chalcidian Peninsula, however, they found no Athenian warships to support their military efforts. After pillaging the Chalcidian Peninsula for several days, and being unable to besiege the Greek cities without the Athenian war machines, the Thracians returned to their homeland after having stolen enormous amounts of gold. In 424 BC, Sitalces died and his realm was subsequently fragmented into several smaller kingdoms.

With the collapse of the Odrysian Kingdom, Perdiccas II was finally able to secure his control over the Kingdom of Macedonia and then decided to side with Sparta during the ongoing Peloponnesian War. In 424 BC, the Macedonians helped the Spartans in conquering the Athenian colony of Amphipolis on the coast of southern Thrace, which had been supplying Athens with large amounts of timber for its naval forces. After Amphipolis came under Spartan control, Athens had no choice but to buy timber from the Macedonians, which helped Perdiccas restore the economy of his devastated realm. During 423 BC, the Macedonian king had to face an internal rebellion led by one of his nobles, named Arrhabaeus, who wanted to separate his dominions from the rest of Macedonia and could count on the military support of several Illyrian tribes. To crush this revolt, Perdiccas asked the Spartans for military help, but what was provided proved insufficient as his forces were crushed at the Battle of Lyncestis. Consequently, having seen that his alliance with Sparta had not brought positive results, the Macedonian king changed sides and started to support Athens. Perdiccas II's successor, Archelaus, remained loyal to Athens during the decisive phase of the Peloponnesian War. For example, after the Athenian navy was completely destroyed during the Sicilian expedition of 415–413 BC, he supplied his allies with massive amounts of timber to build a new fleet. Archelaus also built several new infrastructures in his realm, such as roads and military strongholds, and issued good quality coinage. In addition, he was the first Macedonian king to re-equip his infantrymen according to contemporary Greek models, thereby introducing the hoplites' traditional panoply into his kingdom. It was also during the king's reign that the Macedonian capital of Pella (indeed the only major city of Macedonia) was founded. After Archelaus' assassination, Macedonia reverted to a chaotic political situation that saw the proclamation of several new kings in just a few years, most of who ruled for only a few months or years. Consequently, Macedonia's previous internal stability was soon lost. Royal assassinations were frequent events in Macedonia at this time, the local nobles always being prone to revolt and the Argead dynasty being full of potential pretenders to the throne.

This anarchic political situation only came to an end in 392 BC, when Amyntas III assumed power as the monarch of Macedonia. The father of Philip II and grandfather of Alexander the Great, Amyntas III is today considered as the real founder of the unified Kingdom of Macedonia. A very skilled diplomat, Amyntas formed a network of alliances between his realm and the other powers of the southern Balkans, his allies comprising Athens, Thessaly, the Chalcidian League and the Odrysians. At that time, the major external threat for the Macedonians was the Illyrians, who were trying to expand their dominions southwards. Thanks to Amyntas' diplomatic moves, however, Macedonia retained its territorial integrity and all the nobles of the realm were brought back under direct control of the court in Pella. Amyntas III's direct successor was his eldest son, Alexander II, who had many difficulties in keeping order in Macedonia due to the outbreak of a new civil war which was only resolved by Athens' military intervention in support of Alexander, who was thus able to defeat his rival Pausanias. The new Macedonian king tried to expand his realm's sphere of influence by intervening in the internal politics of Thessaly, which at that time was ravaged by a civil war. The Macedonians occupied a large part of northern Thessaly, but this audacious move was quickly punished by the city of Thebes (at that time the dominant military power of Greece following the demise of Sparta and Athens). After having been defeated by the superior Theban military forces, Alexander II was

Personal equipment of a Macedonian phalangite, including Pilos helmet. (*Photo and copyright by Hetairoi*)

Macedonian foot companions deployed with their pikes in the vertical position. (*Photo and copyright by Hetairoi*)

forced to abandon Thessaly and to become an ally of Thebes. In addition, he had to send his younger brother, Philip (the future father of Alexander the Great), to Thebes as a royal hostage. Alexander II was succeeded by Amyntas III's second son, Perdiccas III, who tried to regain from the Illyrians some lands that had been lost by the Macedonians but was killed during one of his military campaigns. Perdiccas III's sudden death in 359 BC caused a great political upheaval in Pella, with the Macedonian nobles choosing the infant son of the monarch as their new king rather than Philip. However, Philip soon managed to become the tutor and regent of the infant, and some months later, he proclaimed himself king and dethroned his young nephew (who was executed in 335 BC).

Macedonian foot companions deploying themselves into a file. (*Photo and copyright by Hetairoi*)

Chapter 2

The Ascendancy of Macedonia under Philip II

In 359 BC, at the age of 23, Philip II became supreme ruler of Macedonia during the most difficult period in the history of his kingdom. After the sudden death of Perdiccas III, the enemies of the Macedonians had formed a strong military alliance and invaded Philip's new kingdom, taking advantage of the political chaos that reigned in Pella. The Illyrians raided the north-west of Macedonia, while a joint force of Paeonians and Thracians pillaged the eastern half of the state. Meanwhile, the Athenians landed a military contingent just south of Macedonia to support a false pretender to the throne of Pella named Argeus. Pressed by enemies on all sides and being in a very weak military position, Philip had no choice but to use diplomacy to slow down the actions of his most dangerous enemies. He halted the raids of the Paeonians and Thracians by promising to pay them a tribute, thereby gaining precious time to mobilize his forces. At the same time, he married the daughter of the most powerful Illyrian warlord, Bardylis of the Dardanians. Bardylis had been able to unite several southern Illyrian communities into a single kingdom and had defeated the Macedonian army of Perdiccas III; according to ancient sources, Bardylis had killed the Macedonian king with his own hands. Being in no condition to face the Dardanians on equal terms, Philip preferred to form an alliance with them through his marriage. After thus stabilizing the military situation on his northern borders, Philip marched against the 3,000 Athenian hoplites who had landed south of Macedonia and eliminated the pretender Argeus after gaining a decisive victory. In a time of terrible crisis, Philip had been able to preserve the territorial integrity of his realm. However, it was clear to him that he would soon be obliged to fight against the tribes that still represented a threat to the borders of Macedonia. In 358 BC, hostilities resumed between the Macedonians and Illyrians; the latter were still in control of a large portion of northern Macedonia, which was an unacceptable situation for Philip. The young warrior king mobilized every able-bodied man of his realm and marched against Bardylis. The decisive clash of this new war took place in the Erigon Valley, when the Macedonian phalanx was deployed on the battlefield for the first time. The battle ended with a brilliant victory for Philip, the first of his incredible military career, with 7,000 Illyrians killed, including Bardylis. Thanks to this unexpected success, the Macedonians could reconquer the north-western portion of their realm

and establish a new frontier line with the Dardanians along the shores of Lake Ohrid. The new border could be defended much more easily by the Macedonians than the previous one, and remained unchanged for many years. The new phalanx which Philip deployed in battle in the Erigon Valley was the most important product of a series of military reforms that were carried out by the young Macedonian king between late 359 BC and early the following year.

Philip, who had lofty personal ambitions, wanted to transform his realm into a great regional power, and knew that to do so he had to forge an effective and modern military machine. When he ascended to the throne, the Macedonian Army was in a deplorable state, mostly armed as tribal troops without hoplite organization or equipment. The young Macedonian monarch had lived in Thebes as a royal hostage from 368–365 BC, during which he received an excellent military education from two of the most important Greek generals of the time: Epaminondas and Pelopidas. These military leaders had transformed Thebes into the dominant power in Greece, and are still remembered today as great tacticians. They radically reformed hoplite warfare after two centuries of continuity in Greek military tactics. The military guile of Epaminondas and Pelopidas was shown to the whole Hellenic world at the Battle of Leuctra in 371 BC, when the once-mighty Spartan hoplites were crushed by the

A file of Macedonian phalangites with their sarissae in the vertical position. (*Photo and copyright by Hetairoi*)

Macedonian phalangites on the march, transporting their dismantled sarissae on their shoulders. (*Photo and copyright by Hetairoi*)

Thebans. During this clash, one of the most famous in the military history of Ancient Greece, Epaminondas employed some incredibly innovative tactics that were decisive in securing victory. The traditional phalanx formation of the Greek hoplites had a natural tendency to veer to the right during battles, as it was natural for each hoplite to do his best to shelter his unarmed side behind the shield of the fighter located to his right. As a result of this tendency, Greek military commanders always placed their best troops on the right flank of their armies. At Leuctra, for example, the Spartan commander placed his 700 elite Spartiates on the right. Epaminondas, instead, did something completely different. Understanding that he was fighting against a much more numerous enemy and thus risked being easily outflanked, he firstly took the best troops of his army (including the famous Theban 'Sacred Band') and deployed them on his left flank in order to face the Spartiates. He also arranged these soldiers of the left flank in a much more dense formation (fifty ranks deep instead of the usual eight to twelve ranks). As a result, the Thebans not only had their best troops on the left, but also enjoyed a local numerical superiority over the elite Spartiates. Epaminondas also adopted for the first time in Greek military history an oblique formation. Since his right flank was now formed by troops of mediocre quality who were inferior in number to those confronting them, he instructed his hoplites on the right to avoid battle with the enemy and withdraw gradually as the Spartans advanced. In that sector, the Spartan line was much longer than that of the Thebans, so accepting battle there would have led to a Spartan outflanking manoeuvre. The Thebans thus attacked in a way never seen before by the Spartans: their elite left advanced at double speed, while their weak right retreated without fighting. The Spartans had never fought against an enemy in this oblique formation, and had always been victorious thanks to the decisive charge of their elite right wing. Leuctra was a brilliant victory for Epaminondas and Pelopidas, with some 400 of the 700 Spartiates perishing on the field of battle. Crucially, Sparta was unable to replace such severe losses.

While in Thebes, Philip learned everything about their novel tactics from Pelopidas and Epaminondas. He also had the opportunity to study the organization of the victorious Theban forces. Around 395 BC, the army of the Boeotian League, which included that of Thebes, deployed a total of 11,000 hoplites and 1,100 cavalrymen. Such numbers were comparable to those of the contemporary Athenian military forces, but it must be remembered that the Boeotian League was a confederation of several *poleis* guided by Thebes and not a single state. Boeotia was divided into eleven territorial districts, four of which were Thebes' direct possessions; each district elected a supreme military commander (known as a '*boeotarch*') and had to raise 1,100 soldiers (1,000 hoplites and 100 cavalry). Consequently, Thebes alone could field

Macedonian hypaspist; the general appearance is that of a Greek hoplite, with dory spear and hoplon shield. The cuirass was worn only on guard duties by members of the Vanguard Battalion. (*Photo and copyright by Hetairoi*)

Macedonian hypaspist wearing a magnificent example of Attic helmet. (*Photo and copyright by Hetairoi*)

4,000 hoplites and 400 cavalry, a military force comparable to that of the Spartiates. The Theban contingent of the army of the Boeotian League also comprised a special unit of 300 '*epilektoi*' ('chosen soldiers'): the '*Hieros Lochos*' or Sacred Band, probably the most famous military unit of Classical Greece. The 300 hoplites who made up this corps were full-time professional soldiers. They formed the permanent garrison of Thebes and were stationed in the city's strongest fortress, the Cadmeia. The Sacred Band, which was probably created around 378 BC, soon became famous for its excellent training.

While in Thebes, Philip could also study the recent military reforms carried out by the Athenians. At the beginning of the fourth century BC, Iphicrates, an Athenian general who had conducted several campaigns in Thrace, reformed the military forces of his city by changing the panoply of the traditional Greek troop types. He was the first who saw the great potential of the peltasts as a sort of 'medium infantry', who could fight both as light skirmishers and as heavy 'shock' troops according to circumstances on the battlefield. The peltast was the standard Thracian light infantryman, a skirmisher equipped with a crescent-shaped wicker shield (the pelte, from which he took his name) and a couple of throwing javelins. These fighters were able to move very rapidly and were perfectly suited for operating on broken terrain. The Thracian warriors were used to fight as skirmishers, their wars being mostly inter-tribal conflicts that involved the raiding of nearby villages and cattle rustling. They wore no armour and their offensive weapons consisted of javelins, making them perfect for hit-and-run 'guerrilla' tactics and killing their enemies from a distance (for example during ambushes). Their pelte shield was crescent-shaped in order to make the throwing of javelins more easy. Each peltast could throw a javelin over the top of his shield's convex part while protecting his torso behind the concave section. Instead of a helmet, the Thracian peltasts wore a cap made of fox-skin, perfectly suited to the cold temperatures of their homeland's winters thanks to the presence of a pair of earflaps. A square cloak and a long tunic, both very thick, were also worn. The traditional Thracian dress was completed by a pair of fur-lined fawn-skin boots, which were perfect to run on terrain covered with snow. The fur lining hung down in three distinctively Thracian lappets. Initially, the Greek hoplites had great difficulties in fighting against the Thracians, since they moved too slowly to respond effectively to their rapid attacks. Consequently, some Greek commanders started to develop a new category of lighter infantrymen known as *ekdromoi*, who were chosen from the youngest and fittest of the hoplites. They did not wear armour or greaves, since they were expected to run out of their battle lines in order to catch the Thracian peltasts before they could withdraw after having thrown their javelins. The term *ekdromoi*, in fact, simply meant 'out-runners'. Nevertheless, the creation of this new category of 'light hoplites' was not enough by itself to effectively face the Thracians, so the Greeks also had to introduce some peltasts into their own armies. This was initially done by simply recruiting more Thracian mercenaries, since large numbers of them were always available. However, the Greek cities then started to train and equip some of their citizen-soldiers as peltasts rather than as hoplites. In the Greek military system of this time, a peltast was a sort of 'medium' infantryman: they did not have the same traditional dress of the original Thracian peltasts, but did use the same basic equipment, with pelte shield and javelins.

In 391 BC, at the Battle of Lechaeum, the Athenian Iphicrates was able to defeat – for the first time in history – a contingent of Spartan hoplites with just a force of peltasts. Iphicrates had already modified the panoply and tactics of the Athenian peltasts. Instead of the traditional pelte shield, he gave them a large oval shield (always made of wicker), while his new peltasts wore a helmet to protect their head. Offensive weapons now also included a short sword and a short spear, in addition to the usual javelins. Thanks to the larger shield and new helmet, the Iphicratean peltast could fight in close combat against a hoplite. Indeed, thanks to the new sword and spear, the peltast now had more or less the same offensive capabilities as a heavy infantryman. Compared to a hoplite, however, the new peltast was much more mobile, since he wore no body armour. Iphicrates had completed the transition of the peltast from a light infantryman to a medium one. After the positive experience of Lechaeum, the Athenian general also decided to modify the panoply and tactics of the standard hoplite. The large hoplon shield was abandoned in favour of a much smaller and lighter round shield (known as a pelte, like the crescent-shaped one of the peltasts). Furthermore, the metal greaves were discarded, replaced by new leather boots known as 'Iphicratids' from the name of their creator (which were very similar to those worn by the Thracians), while new lighter cuirasses made of quilted linen replaced the older models. Meanwhile, the spear, to compensate the lightening of the defensive equipment, was lengthened up to 3.6 metres. The new small shield could be strapped to the forearm, thus freeing the left hand to help hold the longer spear.

Iphicrates had made the panoply of the peltasts heavier and that of the hoplites lighter. While his military reforms, which were revolutionary for the time, did not save the Athenian Army from its slow decline, they did have a fundamental impact over the future development of the new Macedonian phalanx introduced by Philip II. Philip's phalangites were just an improved version of the Iphicratean hoplites. From the Thebans, meanwhile, the Macedonian monarch had taken the idea of creating a special corps of chosen soldiers – like the Sacred Band – who could perform specific tactical functions on the battlefield.

Before the ascendancy of Philip, the Macedonian Army was mostly known in Greece for the great quality of its cavalry, while its infantry was little more than a poorly equipped and badly trained band of peasants that could not compare to the elite heavy infantry hoplites of the Greek cities. Differently from most of the Greek states, Macedonia had enough plains to breed a large number of horses, which had always enabled the nobles to deploy personal retinues made up of cavalrymen. The weak Macedonian infantry consisted only of lightly armed skirmishers who were not so different from their Illyrian or Thracian enemies, but who were not capable of fighting with the latter's efficiency. The Macedonian infantry clearly needed to be reformed, but importing hoplite warfare to the Kingdom of Macedonia was not a simple matter because the state had no middle class from which the heavy infantry could be recruited. In the early decades of the fourth century BC, especially during the reign of Archelaus (413–399 BC), the Macedonian kings had already started an attempt to reform their infantry forces. For any future confrontation with the armies of the Greek world, the light Macedonian infantry used to fight against the northern tribes of the Balkans would have proved of no military use. The Macedonians thus started to organize and train some of their infantrymen as hoplites. When Philip ascended to the throne of Pella in 359 BC, the Macedonian Army could field 600 cavalry and 10,000 infantry, but only a small portion of the latter were equipped as hoplites, the majority of them still made up of shepherds and farmers who were armed like light infantry skirmishers in the Illyrian or Thracian style. Philip decided to change the situation by transforming his army into a combined force of 'shock' troops, with heavy cavalry and heavy infantry playing a prominent role. As a result, he created two main bodies of new regular troops: the *pezhetairoi* or 'foot companions' and the *heitairoi* or 'horse companions'.

According to Macedonian law, each able-bodied male was available for military service as an infantryman. However, the quality of these foot soldiers, as we have seen, was generally quite poor. In practice, the Macedonian foot soldiers were virtually indistinguishable from their Illyrian or Thracian enemies, and were totally unprepared for a direct confrontation with the Greek hoplites. Philip quickly understood that the only way to defeat his tribal enemies of the north was by creating a superior military force through employing new tactics and equipment that would surprise Macedonia's traditional opponents. Upon starting the reform of his infantry, Philip decided to transform his foot soldiers into Iphicratean hoplites, which he did through the help of Greek mercenary officers who imported the drill and discipline of the Greek citizen armies into the Kingdom of Macedonia. The new *pezhetairoi* infantrymen were the key factor behind Philip's victory over the Illyrians in 358 BC, and thus we can presume that they started to be organized during late 359 BC. The

Macedonian hypaspist with bronze muscle cuirass and Argead Star painted on the hoplon shield. (*Photo and copyright by Athenea Prómakhos*)

Full panoply of Macedonian hypaspist or Greek allied/mercenary hoplite. (*Photo and copyright by Hetairoi*)

pezhetairoi numbered some 9,000 men and were organized into six regiments or *taxeis* of 1,500 men each; a single *taxis* comprised three battalions or *lochoi* with 500 soldiers each. The *lochoi* were usually divided into two blocks of 256 men, known as *syntagmata*, each of which corresponded to a phalanx, with its soldiers being deployed into sixteen files of sixteen men each. It should be noted, however, that the phalanx was a tactical unit and not an administrative one like the *syntagmata*. Each phalanx was divided into sixteen smaller units known as *dekas*, corresponding to the single files of sixteen infantrymen. Each regiment of the foot companions was raised from a different district of Macedonia, from which it took its official denomination, whereas the battalions (*lochoi*) were named after their commanders. In total, with each regiment of the *pezhetairoi* able to deploy six phalanxes, the whole division of the foot companions could field a total of fifty-four phalanxes. Thanks to the introduction of new standard equipment and intensive training, Philip was able to create a new class of professional foot soldiers in a very short time. The foot companions, being raised among the peasants and farmers of his kingdom, comprised men having both a good temperament and excellent physical condition.

Cavalry had always been a secondary element of Greek warfare, since the armies of the various *poleis* generally included very few horsemen (only a few hundred). This was mostly due to two factors: firstly, most Greek territory was covered by mountains or hills and was thus not suitable for breeding large numbers of good quality horses; secondly, only the richest citizens of each *polis* could sustain the expenses needed for maintaining a war horse for a long time. Two areas of Greece were an exception to this general rule: Thessaly and Boeotia, which consisted of flat plains with excellent pasture for horses. As a result, these were the only regions of Greece where cavalry were dominant from a military point of view. The Boeotian *poleis* became increasingly important and populated, which led to the adoption of the urban hoplite military system in Thebes and to a gradual decrease in importance of the Boeotian cavalry.

This did not happen in Thessaly, where the few local cities remained quite isolated and did not acquire great political importance. The Thessalians continued to fight as cavalrymen throughout the Classical period and never adopted the hoplite military system on a large scale. The Thessalian terrain was perfect for rearing cattle and growing grain, which enabled the local aristocrats to grow rich thanks to the export of these important products. The Thessalians, be they aristocrats or commoners, were used to riding from their early childhood, and fought as deadly light cavalry armed with javelins. They did not wear armour, helmet or shield; mobility and speed were the key factors of their tactical success. The Thessalian horsemen were excellent skirmishers who loved to use hit-and-run tactics and to fight from a distance with their throwing weapons. In order to ride more comfortably, the Thessalians developed their own national riding dress during the Classical period, which included a wide-brimmed sun-hat known as a *petasos*, which protected its wearer from heat and dust during the summer months. Over time, a metal version of the *petasos* became popular, a helmet with the same shape as the original sun-hat. Thessalian cavalry also wore a long and enveloping cloak, which was used in combination with a tunic during winter or was worn on the naked body in the summer. Thin cavalry boots, of the same kind employed by all the other Greek horsemen, could be worn; frequently, however, the Thessalians rode barefoot. The Thessalian riding dress became so popular that all the cavalrymen of Greece, even the Athenians, adopted it to look similar to the skilled horsemen of Thessaly. The Thessalian cavalry frequently served outside their region, as mercenaries or allies of the various Greek leagues of cities: having a contingent of Thessalian horsemen often proved a decisive factor in winning a battle. In addition to javelins, Thessalian horsemen also employed a long cavalry lance known as a *kamax*, which was designed to strike enemy infantry while charging and enabled the Thessalians to also act as 'shock' cavalry if needed. Slashing swords could also be carried, especially by the richest individuals. From a political

Greek allied/mercenary hoplite with Chalcidian helmet. (*Photo and copyright by Athenea Prómakhos*)

Greek allied/ mercenary hoplite with Chalcidian helmet. (*Photo and copyright by Athenea Prómakhos*)

point of view, Thessaly was traditionally divided into four tetrarchies or cantons, which formed a loose confederation known as the Thessalian League, guided by a supreme leader (the *tagos*). Each tetrarchy was divided into a number of *kleroi* ('lots'), each of the which provided forty cavalrymen and eighty infantrymen to the Thessalian League for military service. Since Thessaly had 150 *kleroi*, the Thessalian League could deploy a total of 12,000 infantry and 6,000 cavalry. Thessalian infantry comprised a mix of light troops, including a good number of peltasts, but its general quality was not comparable to that of the cavalry. The military organization of Thessaly changed only around 374 BC, when the ambitious Jason of Pherae became the *tagos* of the Thessalian League. Jason abolished the *kleroi* and established cities as the territorial unit from which military contingents were levied. He also introduced a new rhomboid formation for his powerful cavalry, which proved to be unstoppable during attacks and later evolved into the famous wedge employed with enormous success by the Macedonian cavalry.

The Macedonian cavalry, before being reformed by Philip II, had a lot in common with that of the Thessalians since it consisted of a multi-tasking force that could be employed to conduct frontal charges as well as to skirmish with the enemy from a distance. The Macedonian mounted troops were made up of the upper-class inhabitants of the kingdom, who were economically able to maintain excellent war horses. It is interesting to note, however, that a certain number of the cavalrymen were non-nobles who enjoyed the trust and friendship of the Macedonian king and thus had the privilege to serve at Philip's side as his bodyguard. These elite soldiers were the personal retinue of the king, and as such enjoyed a series of privileges. The new regular cavalry of the horse companions created by Philip was organized on eight squadrons known as *ilai*, each of which comprised 200 horsemen, with the exception of the elite unit called the *basilike ile* (Royal Squadron) or *agema* (Vanguard). The latter squadron, which originated from the personal retinue of the monarch, had 400 men and acted as Philip's mounted bodyguard. Together, the eight squadrons of the horse companions were considered an independent cavalry regiment, with each squadron divided into two sections of 100 men each, except for the *agema* that had four sections. Each section was in turn divided into two *tetrarchiai* of fifty soldiers. Like the infantry regiments of the foot companions, the *ilai* were recruited on a territorial basis from the various districts of the kingdom. They were named after their commanders and could be sometimes grouped together into a larger cavalry formation of three or four squadrons, which was known as a *hipparchy*. With the ascendancy of Philip II, the internal composition of the Royal Squadron underwent a dramatic change. Unlike the other 'line' units, it started to be formed solely by aristocrats from the most important noble families of Macedonia. These new

Greek allied/mercenary hoplite with Pilos helmet. (*Photo and copyright by Athenea Prómakhos*)

Macedonian light infantryman with Pilos helmet and pelte round shield. (*Photo and copyright by Hetairoi*)

'personal friends of the king', or *philoi*, were named for life by the monarch and thus were extremely loyal to Philip, who had the *agema* under his direct command. After increasing his cavalry from 600 to 1,800 horsemen in a relatively short time, Philip re-equipped them with cuirasses and helmets, the new horse companions thereby becoming a contingent of 'shock' cavalry designed to conduct frontal charges.

After the end of the Peloponnesian War, most of the Greek cities started to organize permanent military units formed by professional soldiers. These chosen fighters, who remained on active service in times of peace, were commonly known as *epilektoi* ('picked soldiers'). They were usually chosen from the wealthiest and fittest of the younger citizens and were freed from all their public duties in order to perform as full-time soldiers. They trained on a regular basis and were maintained at public expense by the state. In most of the Greek cities, such picked soldiers numbered no more than 300 or 400. This was the case with the most famous of all the *epilektoi* units, the Sacred Band of Thebes, which comprised 300 elite fighters. In case of full-scale war, the *epilektoi* of each city formed the nucleus of professional soldiers around which the rest of the army would be assembled. The contingents of picked soldiers became extremely popular during the fourth century BC, when most of the Greek citizens started to consider compulsory military service in a negative light.

After completing the first phase of his military reforms, which saw the creation of the foot companions and of the horse companions, Philip II decided to raise his own Macedonian regiment of *epilektoi*, the Royal Hypaspists. The Greek word 'hypaspist' meant 'shield-bearer' and was used to identify this new category of soldiers because they carried large hoplite shields, different from the foot companions who were equipped with the smaller pelte shield designed by Iphicrates for his hoplites. Philip decided to create the hypaspists, elite light infantrymen equipped with the traditional hoplite shield but no armour, in order to have a highly mobile and flexible unit that could link the foot companions with the horse companions on the battlefield. When the cavalry advanced, the hypaspists had to move forward rapidly to keep up with the horsemen. The heavy infantry of the phalanxes were too slow in their close formations to perform such tactical manoeuvres. The idea of creating fast-moving infantry that could support the cavalry in its attacks was not a new phenomenon: a similar category of foot soldiers already existed in the Hellenic world, the *hamippoi*, created by the tyrant Gelon of Syracuse before the outbreak of the Persian Wars. The Syracusan army, like that of Macedonia, contained a large number of excellent cavalrymen, but unlike the situation in Greece, they were considered as more important than the hoplites and made up an elite force. During the period from 490–480 BC, while Gelon was tyrant of Syracuse, the Greeks of Sicily fought against the Carthaginians who were expanding on the island.

During this conflict, in order to effectively support his numerous horsemen in the clashes with the Carthaginian cavalry, Gelon introduced a new category of light infantrymen known as *Hippodromoi Psiloi*, light infantrymen who ran alongside the cavalry. These troops, who would later be simply known as *hamippoi*, performed a specific tactical function: each of them had to go into battle running behind the horse of a cavalryman, holding on to the tail or mane of the animal. In battle, the *hamippoi* slipped underneath the horses of the enemy cavalry and ripped their bellies open, for which they were equipped with a short dagger and were trained to run for long distances with the cavalry. The regiment of the Royal Hypaspists, modelled after the *hamippoi*, was raised from the personal retainers of Philip II who had already been included in the new foot companions. The foot equivalent of the mounted Royal Saquadron, the unit had a larger establishment than the normal infantry *taxeis*, comprising 3,000 elite soldiers organized into six battalions (*lochoi*) with 500 soldiers each. One of the *lochoi*, known as the Vanguard Battalion, had a special status and consisted of 500 picked men who were selected out of the whole Macedonian Army for their height. The chosen *lochos* guarded the king's tent on campaign and always took the place of honour in the Macedonian battle-line. According to ancient sources, the hypaspists also acted as a sort of military police for the Macedonian Army, being tasked with keeping order in the ranks of the various units and with preventing desertions.

After completing his military reforms and testing his new units in battle in the Erigon Valley, Philip II understood that the quality of his troops could enable him to transform Macedonia into the superpower of the Hellenic world. The individual southern *poleis* were tired of war, lacked manpower and were politically divided. The first target of Philip's new expansionist policy was Thessaly, which had been recently organized as a semi-centralized state by Jason of Pherae. After Jason's death, however, Thessaly was ravaged by bloody civil wars that saw the participation of Macedonia and Thebes. In 358 BC, Philip launched an invasion of Thessaly in order to install a new government that would be favourable to him. The following year, the Macedonians moved against Amphipolis, a strategically important Greek city that was located between the Chalcidian Peninsula and the southern coastline of Thrace. Amphipolis controlled a countryside that was rich in gold and was of strategic importance for Athens, so when the Macedonians attacked, the Athenians supported the city (which had previously been an Athenian colony). Despite the arrival of Athenian reinforcements, Amphipolis was conquered by Philip, who then concluded a formal alliance with the Greek *poleis* of the Chalcidian League. In exchange for Macedonian military protection, the Chalcidian League ceded the

Macedonian light infantryman with Chalcidian helmet and small round shield. (*Photo and copyright by Athenea Prómakhos*)

Macedonian light infantryman throwing his javelin. (*Photo and copyright by Athenea Prómakhos*)

city of Potidea to Philip, who continued to expand southwards by besieging and conquering Pydna.

From 356–346 BC, most of the Greek cities were involved in a new conflict, commonly known as the Third Sacred War because it was caused by the refusal of Phocis to pay a fine imposed by the Temple of Apollo at Delphi (the most important religious institution of Greece). The conflict was mostly fought between Phocis and Thebes, the latter city controlling the decisions taken by the Temple of Apollo at Delphi and using them for political gain. Phocis was supported by Athens and Sparta, while Thebes could count on the help of Locris and Macedonia.

Philip intervened in the Third Sacred War only to establish a firm Macedonian hegemony over Thessaly, which was full of precious natural resources and linked Macedonia to central Greece. The Thessalian cavalry was of excellent quality, and could count on the support of large light infantry contingents. Philip wanted to absorb the Thessalians into his army and to expand his domains over the fertile plains of Thessaly. He occupied most of Thessaly with his army, but was defeated by a substantial military force sent by the Phocians. After this temporary setback, the Macedonians reorganized and invaded Thessaly again. The new campaign ended with Philip's great victory at the Battle of Crocus Field, which was fought by the Macedonians against an alliance comprising Athens and Phocis. After this clash, Philip was appointed *tagos* of Thessaly and thus became the supreme ruler of the region, which was effectively transformed into a vassal state of Macedonia. In 349 BC, Philip attacked his former allies of the Chalcidian League and defeated them after a brilliant campaign, all the cities of the League thereafter accepting the Macedonian king as their overlord, except for Olynthos (the most important of the Chalcidian *poleis*) that continued to resist. The Macedonians defeated the Olynthians in two subsequent pitched battles and then started besieging their city, which was quickly conquered and razed by Philip, who annexed the whole territory of the Chalcidian League to his realm. Athens was unable to send substantial reinforcements to help Olynthos because during the same period a coalition of anti-Athenian *poleis* had been formed on the island of Euboea. Fearing that the Macedonians could use this event to their advantage, the Athenians landed an army on Euboea to bring the region back into their sphere of influence. The Athenian expedition, however, was a complete failure, so the Euboean cities also became allies of Philip. In 346 BC, with neither Thebes nor Phocis able to prevail, the Third Sacred War finally came to an end, and Macedonia signed a peace treaty with Athens. The only real victor of the conflict had been Philip, who had used it to conquer most of northern Greece and Thessaly. The terms of the peace treaty were particularly favourable for Macedonia, since they formally recognized Philip's kingdom as the most important player in the Greek political scene. In less than fifteen years, the ambitious Macedonian monarch had transformed his kingdom from a land of barbarians into a major military power.

After these events, it became clear that the future of Greece would be decided by a clash between Macedonia and Athens. The Athenians had not forgotten the fall of Amphipolis, and had decided to fight against the Macedonian 'tyrant king' with all the resources at their disposal. Instigated by the famous orator Demosthenes and his vigorous 'Philippics' political speeches, the Athenian government tried to form a large anti-Macedonian military alliance. During 340 and 339 BC, Philip besieged

Illyrian/Thracian light infantryman with Chalcidian helmet and crescent-shaped pelte shield (left), together with a Thessalian light cavalryman wearing a petasos sun hat and throwing javelins (right). (*Photo and copyright by Athenea Prómakhos*)

two important *poleis* located near the Dardanelles and the Hellespont: Perinthos and Byzantion. The Athenians sent substantial naval forces to support Byzantion, which helped the city resist the besieging Macedonians. At that time the Kingdom of Macedonia did not have a military fleet, since Philip had only recently conquered

Thessalian light infantryman with petasos sun hat. (*Photo and copyright by Hetairoi*)

the Chalcidian Peninsula and there had been no time to build a significant number of warships. As a result, the Athenians had complete control of the sea and could send massive amounts of supplies to the besieged cities. Eventually, unable to obtain any significant success, the Macedonians decided to abandon the sieges of Perinthos and Byzantion in order to move directly against Athens. Philip had decided to organize a final and decisive invasion of Greece so that he could become the supreme overlord of the Hellenic world. Realizing that the political situation was changing in a dramatic way and that Macedonia could effectively conquer the whole of Greece, Thebes decided to put aside its differences with Athens to join in the desperate struggle that was about to be fought. At that time the Theban forces were still considered the best in Greece; if supported by Athens and other allies, Thebes felt it could halt the Macedonians. After all, Philip had been instructed in the art of war by the great Theban military leaders of the previous decades.

The decisive battle between the Macedonians and the Greeks was fought at Chaeronea in 338 BC, where some 32,000 Macedonian soldiers commanded by Philip and by his young son Alexander (the future Alexander the Great) faced 35,000 Greeks (mostly Thebans and Athenians, supported by some minor allied contingents). The Greeks fought with enormous courage, but were utterly defeated. While Alexander's role in the battle was important in securing victory for his father, in reality the Greeks were defeated by the superiority of the new Macedonian phalanx. The Thebans resisted as long as they could, but their glorious Sacred Band was completely annihilated: not one of the 300 elite hoplites survived, including the unit's commander. After the Battle of Chaeronea, Philip treated the Thebans very harshly and destroyed their military potential, whereas the Athenians were spared because the Macedonian monarch needed their fleet for his future campaigns. All the Greek cities were obliged to accept Macedonian suzerainty, and the most important ones had to house a Macedonian garrison inside their walls. The Spartans, who had not taken part in the war, initially rejected Philip's requests but were in no condition to fight alone against the Macedonian king, who ravaged their territories and forced them to accept Macedonia as the ruling power of Greece.

In 337 BC, Philip created the League of Corinth, a confederation of states comprising most of the Greek cities (except Sparta) that was guided by Macedonia. This would provide Philip with large military contingents in case of war and participate in subsequent military campaigns conducted by Macedonia. After having conquered Greece, the ambitious Philip was already planning to invade the immense territories of the Persian Empire. Persia had represented a serious military menace for Greece for centuries, and still controlled the Hellenic cities on the western coast of Asia Minor. After Chaeronea, Philip had presented himself as the defender of all Greeks,

Thessalian light infantryman; most of the foot soldiers from the region of Thessaly were equipped as peltasts. (*Photo and copyright by Hetairoi*)

Personal equipment of a Macedonian light infantryman, including Pilos helmet. (*Photo and copyright by Hetairoi*)

Light infantryman's round shield made of wicker and throwing javelins. (*Photo and copyright by Athenea Prómakhos*)

and thus the emancipation of the Hellenic cities in Asia was a perfect *casus belli* to initiate his invasion of Persian territory. In 336 BC a Macedonian expeditionary force of 10,000 soldiers landed in Asia Minor, being welcomed by the local Greeks who revolted against their Persian governors. However, before any effective fighting could take place between the Macedonians and the Persians, Philip II was assassinated by one of his bodyguards.

Chapter 3

The Rise of Alexander the Great

Alexander of Macedonia was born in Pella, probably on 20 July 356 BC, the son of Philip II and Olympias, the king's fourth wife. Olympias was the daughter of Neoptolemus I, king of Epirus, and had been married by Philip largely for political reasons. By 350 BC, Macedonia had become much more hellenized than the Kingdom of Epirus, and Olympias was considered a barbarian by those inside the court at Pella. She belonged to a royal family that claimed to descend from Achilles and practised a series of religious rites that were not part of the traditional Hellenic cults. The birth of Alexander was accompanied, according to ancient sources, by a series of symbolic events: the Temple of Arthemis in Ephesus, one of the Seven Wonders of the World and the most important religious site of the Greeks in Asia Minor, was destroyed by a violent fire; Macedonian military forces deployed on the northern border of their kingdom obtained a victory over the Illyrians and Paeonians; and Philip II's horses won the most important race at the Olympic Games. The Macedonian monarch, who was besieging the city of Potidea at the time of Alexander's birth, was greatly impressed by these 'signals' that were interpreted as warning the whole Hellenic world about the birth of his son. During the following years, Alexander was educated like all the young Macedonian nobles of his time: he learned how to ride, fight, hunt, read and play the lyre. Since his early childhood, Alexander had a special passion for horses, as confirmed by the famous episode of his first encounter with the horse Bucephalus. When Alexander was just 10 years old, a Thessalian merchant came to the royal court at Pella with a magnificent black stallion which refused to be mounted. All the members of the Macedonian court who tried to ride him failed. The young Alexander, realizing that the horse was nervous because it feared its own shadow, asked permission to tame Bucephalus in front of his father, Philip. To the astonishment of all those present, the boy was able to calm down the horse and to start riding him within a few minutes: from that day Bucephalus became Alexander's most loyal companion. Philip, greatly impressed by his son's courage, declared: 'My boy, you must find a kingdom big enough for your ambitions; Macedonia is too small for you.'

The military training of the Macedonian prince was particularly harsh, since he was treated like all the other noble youths of the court and was assigned to an

Thracian warrior with Chalcidian helmet and rhomphaia sickle. (*Photo and copyright by Ancient Thrace*)

Thracian peltast with crescent-shaped shield and throwing javelins. (*Photo and copyright by Ancient Thrace*)

implacable tutor named Leonidas (a relative of his mother). Alexander trained for several hours every day, learning how to endure any kind of hardship and being instructed in battle tactics and the use of all kinds of weapons. Hunting was another fundamental component of the prince's education, as it was a very important activity for all Macedonians. Hunts were seen as similar to battles, helping participants to learn how to act rapidly under pressure. Alexander loved hunting and showed his personal courage on several occasions while dealing with wild beasts. It was still possible at that time to find lions in Macedonia and the rest of Greece, and killing one of the beasts was seen as a sign of great audacity. Philip, however, had the intention of transforming Alexander into the future supreme ruler of all the Greeks, and wanted to educate him in all the disciplines that represented the excellence of Greek civilization. The prince was not going to grow up as a barbarian Macedonian aristocrat, devoted only to riding and hunting: he had to learn everything about Greek arts and philosophy in order to one day be able to rule the whole Hellenic world. Desiring his son to have the best possible tutors, Philip contracted the greatest Greek philosopher and educator of his time, Aristotle, to help educate Alexander. Aristotle's lessons were also attended by several other young Macedonian nobles of the same age as Alexander, who became the closest personal friends of the prince. Some years later, when the Macedonian Army invaded Asia, these inexperienced aristocrats would all become generals and would play a crucial role in Alexander's incredible victories. They included Hephaistion, the prince's best friend. Under the intelligent guidance of Aristotle, Alexander developed a passion for Homer's epics and in particular for the *Iliad*; he considered himself as a 'new Achilles' who was destined to conquer Asia for the Greeks.

At the age of 16, Alexander was nominated regent of Macedonia and heir apparent to the throne. At that time, Philip was far away with most of his army fighting against the city of Byzantion. During Philip's absence, one of the Thracian tribes that had previously accepted Macedonian suzerainty revolted against Macedonia. Consequently, Alexander was forced to face the first emergency of his long military career. The Thracian political scene was at the time dominated by four main kingdoms, which had emerged from the collapse of the former Odrysian realm. Understanding that the political fragmentation of the Thracians could be used to his advantage, Philip had invaded southern Thrace in 347 BC but was unable to secure a decisive victory. The Thracians, like the Paeonians and Illyrians, proved to be tough enemies for the Macedonians with their unique combat skills and knowledge of the territory over which the campaign was fought. During the following years, Philip conducted several wars against the Thracian tribes, and by 341 BC most of his initial objectives had been accomplished. The Thracians no longer represented a serious menace to the stability of his kingdom, and he was able to annex southern Thrace to his realm. In 340 BC, however, one of the tribes rebelled against Macedonia, and Alexander, despite his young age, reacted rapidly and moved against the Thracians with the few troops that were at his disposal. The revolt was crushed and the rebellious tribe was expelled forever from its home territory. Alexander repopulated their lands with Macedonian and Greek colonists, and founded a new city named after himself: Alexandropolis. During the following years, dozens of cities named after Alexander would be founded in every corner of Asia.

In 339 BC, Philip campaigned on the northern borders of his kingdom to repulse a large incursion by the Scythians, who had crossed the Danube. The mighty river marked a 'border of civilizations' between the southern peoples of the Balkans and the nomadic tribes living in the north, such as the Scythians. They were excellent horsemen and deadly archers, and could travel enormous distances in just a few days while pillaging any settlements they encountered along the way. Philip's campaign against them was indecisive, and when the Macedonians were marching back home they were ambushed by Thracians seeking revenge for their recent defeat. The tribesmen of the Triballi attacked and defeated the Macedonians, with Philip being badly wounded in the clash. The Macedonian king did not have the time to launch a punitive campaign against the Triballi after this setback, as he was organizing the invasion of Greece. Shortly before this took place, while his father was mobilizing the Macedonian forces, Alexander had to face a minor incursion by the Illyrians, which he was able to easily repulse.

When Philip invaded Greece in 338 BC, Alexander was with him as the commander of the Macedonian cavalry. During the previous few years, fighting against the Thracians and Illyrians, Alexander had demonstrated that he was a capable military commander. Subsequently, at the decisive Battle of Chaeronea in Boeotia, Alexander was the first to break the Theban line at the head of the horse companions, and thus played a prominent role in the great victory that was obtained by the Macedonians. After Chaeronea, Alexander went to Thebes with the ashes of the Theban soldiers who had been killed during the battle and delivered them, with full honours, to the authorities of the city. This act of clemency was greatly appreciated by the Thebans and all the other Greeks, who were won over by the great personal charisma of Alexander. The young prince was quite different to his 'rude' father and had a passion for Greek culture. He was not just a man of war; he was also a man of art and philosophy. After conquering Greece, Philip and Alexander returned to Macedonia. However, something had changed in the relationship between father and son. The king took a new wife, Cleopatra Eurydice, the niece of Attalus, one of his best generals. The new matrimonial union could have produced a new heir to the throne

Thracian tribal peltast. (*Photo and copyright by Ancient Thrace*)

Thracian peltast wearing a zeira cloak. (*Photo and copyright by Ancient Thrace*)

who would have been in a stronger position politically than Alexander. Alexander was only half-Macedonian, while any son of Philip and his new wife would have been a Macedonian of pure blood.

Irritated by his father's decisions and after feuding with Attalus over Philip's marriage, Alexander left Pella with his mother and went in exile to Epirus. He later moved to Illyria, where he was welcomed as a guest by the local warlords, before returning to Pella after some months. Meanwhile, Cleopatra Eurydice had given birth to a daughter and not to a son; as a result, at least for the moment, Alexander remained the only legitimate heir of Philip II. There was, however, the real risk that Philip could still generate a new rival for Alexander or that he could marry another younger wife. Understanding that this was the last chance for her son to become ruler of Macedonia, Olympias organized a plot against Philip that culminated in his assassination in 336 BC. Alexander probably played no active part in the conspiracy, but was well aware of its existence. Pausanias, the bodyguard who killed Philip, was executed by Alexander's friends before he could talk and accuse Olympias of having organized the plot. Meanwhile, the Macedonian court and nobles acclaimed Alexander as their king. Olympias' plan had worked perfectly, but Alexander was very young – he was only 20 – and still needed to consolidate his power by eliminating all potential rivals. The son of Perdiccas III, who had been kept alive for many years by Philip, was executed, as was Cleopatra Eurydice and her young daughter. Attalus, who was in command of the Macedonian forces that Philip had despatched to Asia Minor, was also killed.

While these events took place, the various cities and tribes that had been submitted by the Macedonians during Philip's campaigns rose up in revolt against Alexander. Many of their political leaders were convinced that the new king was too young to rule the territories conquered by his father. Athens, Thebes, Thessaly and the Thracians all rebelled against Alexander. However, the young monarch mobilized his cavalry and moved rapidly and decisively to restore order in his dominions. He first attacked the Thessalians, finding them encamped in a strategic pass located between Mount Olympos and Mount Ossa. In order to surprise his enemies, Alexander ordered some of the horse companions to ride over Mount Ossa and deploy in the rear of the Thessalians. The Thessalians, seeing that there was no chance of victory for them, decided to surrender and joined the Macedonian forces. After regaining control of Thessaly and most of Greece, the young king turned his attention towards Thrace. In the spring of 335 BC, he mounted a full-scale invasion to defeat the Triballi, who were his main opponents in the region. The Thracians were superior to Alexander's light troops, but the phalangites and heavy cavalry of the Macedonian Army were unbeatable in battle. Alexander thus obtained a clear victory over the Thracians

Thracian warrior armed with kopis sword. (*Photo and copyright by Ancient Thrace*)

Thracian peltast with one of his people's traditional symbols painted on the external surface of the shield. (*Photo and copyright by Athenea Prómakhos*)

during a bloody pitched battle. After crushing the Triballi and forcing them to move north of the Danube, Alexander attacked the Getae in another sector of the northern border. The Getae were a people of Thracian stock, but from a cultural point of view they had a strong Scythian influence. Their forces included heavily armoured horsemen and mounted archers like those of the Scythians. Alexander realized that in order to crush the Getae he had to cross the Danube. He was the first Macedonian monarch to attempt such an audacious move, but it paid off and the Getae were decisively defeated and obliged to move north into the territory of the Scythians.

During his brilliant northern campaign of 335 BC, Alexander came into contact with Celtic communities that had been living in the heart of the Balkans for many decades. These tribes were particularly impressed by the military achievements of the Macedonian king and had a positive attitude towards him, since the Thracians defeated by Alexander were their enemies. After his victory over the Getae, Alexander encamped near the Danube with his army and received embassies sent by all the peoples of the region, including those of the Celts. All the local tribes agreed to submit, at least formally, to the Macedonian king. Thanks to Arrian, a formidable ancient source, we know some interesting details about the meeting that took place between Alexander and the Celtic ambassadors. In the words of the Greek historian, the Celts, 'men of haughty demeanour and tall in proportion', came to the Macedonian camp with no intention to submit, merely to recognize Alexander as a capable military leader. The Celtic delegation wanted to offer their people's friendship and proposed an agreement with Alexander that would be positive for both sides. While the Balkan Celts hoped to avoid war with the Macedonians, they had no intention of discussing peace terms from a position of weakness. However, Alexander had different ideas, considering himself as the descendant of Achilles rather than a simple monarch. In order to test the temperament of the Celts, of whom he knew little, the young king asked their representatives what they feared most in the world. He expected their response would have been along the lines of: 'You, great Alexander!' Yet the Celts surprised him with an answer that perfectly reflected their mentality: 'We fear only that the sky falls and crushes us or that the earth opens and swallows us or that the sea rises and overwhelms us.' In essence, what the Celts were saying was that they feared nothing except the power of nature. Initially, Alexander was infuriated by this response, but he quickly came to understand that the Celts could not have answered any differently: they were a people of free and courageous warriors, the kind of men he had always admired. As a result, a peace treaty was indeed concluded between the Macedonians and the Celts that was positive for both sides. Alexander proclaimed himself as the friend of the Celts and promised that he would never invade their lands.

Thracian peltast with alopekis cap and embades boots. (*Photo and copyright by Athenea Prómakhos*)

Thracian tribal peltasts equipped with crescent-shaped shields and throwing javelins. (*Photo and copyright by Ancient Thrace*)

Before returning south, the young Macedonian king also marched into Illyria and defeated two local rulers who were preparing to resume their raids against Macedonia. In an extremely rapid and effective campaign, Alexander had been able to secure the northern borders of his realm and defeated the two most powerful Thracian tribes;

the Danube now marked the frontier between Macedonian territorial possessions and the barbarian northern lands. The Macedonians were thus free to turn their attention towards Greece and the Persian Empire, since their traditional enemies in the Balkans had now been decisively defeated. Alexander next attacked Thebes to raze it to the ground in order to terrorize all the other Greeks and secure his dominance over the League of Corinth. The Macedonians destroyed Thebes in a rapid campaign, with a level of violence that had never before been seen in Greece: nothing remained of the glorious city, and the Theban lands were divided among the other Boeotian *poleis*. Alexander had erased from history one of the most important Greek cities. Athens, fearing they would be the next in line to face destruction at the hands of the Macedonians, surrendered to Alexander without a fight. In the few months since ascending the throne, the new Macedonian king had crushed all rebellions against his rule and restored order in the vast dominions conquered by his father. He was now ready to start his preparations for the invasion of the Persian Empire.

The army with which Alexander landed in Asia Minor had been forged by Philip II. It comprised the three main components already described above: the foot companions, the horse companions and the hypaspists. However, some new elements had recently been added to the Macedonian military forces, while the existing ones had been modified. Consequently, before describing the early phases of Alexander's campaigns in Asia, it is necessary to provide a detailed overview of the Macedonian Army's general organization under Alexander. In addition to the combatants, the Macedonian forces also comprised two special units that, while small, performed important specific duties: the Royal Bodyguard and the Royal Pages. The Royal Bodyguard, for which the Greek name was *somatophylax*, consisted of just seven men drawn from the most important families of the Macedonian aristocracy. These acted both as personal protectors of the king and as high-ranking military officers, holding important command positions in the Macedonian Army. As a result, this small unit functioned as a sort of staff corps that collaborated with the king during his daily activities. As we have seen, Philip was killed by one his bodyguards: this confirms the great importance that the small *somatophylax* had in the Macedonian Army, since its members could decisively influence the behaviour and decisions of the monarch. But before becoming part of the Royal Bodyguard, a Macedonian noble had to serve in the other special unit, the Royal Pages.

Like the *somatophylax*, the Royal Pages were created by Philip II during his reign. According to Macedonian law, all the able-bodied sons of the Macedonian nobility who reached adolescence had to be enrolled into the Royal Pages. This corps worked like a military academy, and its members could be compared to modern cadets since they received some basic military training in its ranks. The future commanders of the Macedonian Army were all educated inside this informal military school, where they learned the basics of military strategy as well as of other disciplines (including philosophy and music). The Royal Pages also regularly practised hunting and sports, thus receiving the same kind of education that was given to Alexander. The period of service spent into the ranks of the Royal Pages was also used to inculcate obedience and deference into the noble youth of Macedonia. Indeed, the young aristocrats were called upon to perform menial duties that were not so different from those of the court's slaves. Historically, the nobility of Macedonia had always been a very turbulent one, so Philip tried to control its secessionist ambitions by influencing the aristocrats from childhood. The members of the Royal Pages can also be seen as hostages for the Macedonian royal family: being forced to live at court in Pella, they served as a strong guarantee of their parents' loyalty towards the Argead dynasty. Upon leaving the Royal Pages, the young aristocrats would either become members of the Royal Bodyguard or enter the ranks of the elite Vanguard Battalion (which was part of the Royal Hypaspists).

At the beginning of Alexander's reign, the *pezhetairoi* heavy infantry comprised a total of 9,000 soldiers, organized into six regiments or *taxeis* of 1,500 men each, with a single *taxis* having three battalions or *lochoi* with 500 soldiers each. The *lochoi* were usually divided into two blocks of 256 men, known as *syntagmata*, each of which corresponded to a phalanx, being deployed into sixteen files of sixteen men each. Each phalanx was divided into sixteen smaller units known as *dekas*, corresponding to the single files of sixteen infantrymen. Each regiment of the foot companions was raised from a different district of Macedonia, from which it took its official denomination, but the *lochoi* were named after their commanders. In total, considering that each regiment of the *pezhetairoi* could deploy six phalanxes, the whole division of the foot companions could field a total of fifty-four phalanxes. Once levied to become part of the foot companions, a Macedonian infantryman could not leave the ranks of his unit and could be removed from his military duties only if discarded by the king. All the phalangites received no pay for their services and had to obey their officers without any hesitation. Each *dekas* of sixteen men was commanded by a senior officer who served in the front rank and also had two junior officers, comparable to modern NCOs, who were placed one at the rear and one in the centre of their *dekas*. These were tasked with steadying the ranks and maintaining cohesion inside their file. Each *lochos* had its own independent commander, known as a *lochagos*, plus five supernumerary soldiers (*ektaktoi*) who performed vital roles: one herald or *stratokerux*, one signalman (*semeiophoros*), one bugler (*salpingtes*), one aide (*hyperetes*) and one file-closer (*ouragos*). All these specialized soldiers supported the *lochagos* in his command

Thracian light infantry skirmisher armed with a curved knife. (*Photo and copyright by Ancient Thrace*)

Thracian boot of the embades type, worn by many light infantrymen of the Macedonian Army. (*Photo and copyright by Ancient Thrace*)

functions and were essential to the correct functioning of their battalion. The herald had to transmit the orders of the *lochagos* to the officers commanding each *dekas*, while the signalman used a codified system of signals to transmit simpler and more immediate orders. The bugler transmitted orders by playing his instrument so that it could be heard by all the other battalions of an infantry *taxis*. The aide supported the *lochagos* in all his functions, acting as the link between him and the common soldiers, and finally the file-closer was tasked with killing any phalangites who tried to abandon their file during combat and was thus charged with preventing desertions. Audial and visual communications were therefore absolutely fundamental to the transmitting of orders (especially in the dust and din of a pitched battle). Above the *lochagos*, each infantry regiment was commanded by a superior officer known as a *strategos*, whose rank was comparable to that of a modern general. Generally speaking, Alexander appointed only his best and most experienced commanders to the rank of *strategos*.

Under Alexander, the hypaspists, elite light infantrymen equipped with the traditional hoplite shield but wearing no armour, were still some 3,000 strong. They were organized into six *lochoi* of 500 men each. One of these units, known as the Vanguard Battalion, had a special status and consisted of 500 picked men who were selected out of the whole Macedonian Army for their height. The chosen *lochos* guarded the king's tent on campaign and always took the place of honour in the Macedonian battle-line. The members of the Vanguard Battalion, unlike the other hypaspists, were all members of the Macedonian nobility and had been trained in the Royal Pages' military academy. The Regiment of Royal Hypaspists had its own independent commander, known as the *archihypaspistes*, who was chosen by the king from the most experienced and loyal officers of the Macedonian Army. Tactically, Alexander employed the hypaspists to perform the same specific duties for which they had been organized by Philip II: they were a highly mobile and flexible unit linking the foot companions with the horse companions on the battlefield. When the cavalry advanced, the hypaspists moved forward rapidly to keep up with the horsemen, thereby avoiding the formation of dangerous gaps between the heavy infantry and heavy cavalry. According to ancient sources, the hypaspists also acted as military policemen, being tasked with keeping order in the ranks of the various units. The Vanguard Battalion also had to provide detachments to permanently guard the person of the king and his personal possessions.

It is important to remember that the Macedonian infantry did not comprise only the heavy regiments of the foot companions and the elite Royal Hypaspists; there were also substantial contingents of foreign and light infantrymen, each with their own peculiar characteristics. When Alexander attacked the Persian Empire, his army included 7,000 Greek heavy infantry sent by the League of Corinth. This large allied corps was formed by several autonomous contingents, each of which was sent by one of the Greek cities that were part of the League. Each Greek city-state was required to contribute to the Macedonian war effort according to its available resources. The Greek heavy infantry contingents were all made up of professional *epilektoi* soldiers, since the traditional hoplite military system had practically disappeared from most of the *poleis*. Each Greek contingent served under its own officers, but the whole body of 7,000 Greek infantry was under the control of a Macedonian supreme commander. In addition to the infantry sent by the League of Corinth, the Macedonian Army included a large number of mercenary Greek foot soldiers, who were mostly employed as garrison troops during the conquest of the Persian Empire, stationed in the newly occupied provinces of Asia while the army advanced further east. The Macedonian officers did not have a very high opinion of their Greek mercenaries, who could be unreliable and prone to revolt if not paid regularly. Despite this, once in Asia Minor, Alexander recruited several hundred more Greek mercenaries who had been part of the Persian Army. The manpower available in Macedonia and Greece was quite limited, so the only way for Alexander to enlarge his infantry was to attract more mercenaries from all available sources. At the Battle of Gaugamela, Alexander deployed two entire infantry regiments made up of mercenaries: the first of these comprised 5,000 men, while the second had 4,000 soldiers (bringing the total of Greek foot soldiers in the Macedonian Army to 16,000 allies or mercenaries). The first regiment had elite status and its members were known as *archaioi* (veterans) because they were the original mercenaries who had departed Greece at the beginning of the Asian campaign. The second unit was known as the Achaean regiment, as its 4,000 men were all recruited in Achaea (one of the poorest regions of Greece, famous for exporting mercenaries throughout the Mediterranean). All the Greek infantry, be they allies or mercenaries, were equipped as traditional hoplites and not as phalangites.

The light infantry of the Macedonian Army were known as the *psiloi*. While less famous than the phalangites or hoplites, they had been a regular component of Greek armies for some two centuries. Originally, the *psiloi* comprised the poorest citizens of each *polis*, who could not afford the complete hoplite panoply. During military campaigns, most of them went to the field of battle in their ordinary clothes, with no armour, and were equipped with rudimentary weapons (javelins and stones) and had no specific training. These light infantrymen, with no particular specialization, played only a secondary role during battles, as due to their lack of training and minimal equipment they did not represent a serious threat to the heavily armed and armoured hoplites. When peltasts began appearing in Greek armies, the importance of the *psiloi* waned. The peltasts were superior to

Macedonian psilos light infantryman, wearing sun hat and armed with javelins. The psilos light infantry were poorly equipped, with no armour or shield. (*Photo and copyright by Athenea Prómakhos*)

Macedonian psilos light infantryman armed with a stone. Note the practice of using the fur of a wild animal as a form of rudimentary shield. (*Photo and copyright by Athenea Prómakhos*)

all the other light infantrymen thanks to their use of the pelte shield. The *psiloi* had regained some importance during the Peloponnesian War, when Athens was obliged to employ all available citizens in combat. They could be useful during siege operations, for example to defend the walls of a fortified city, or when employed as explorers/skirmishers. Since they wore no helmet and did not have any armour or shield, the *psiloi* could move quite rapidly on every kind of terrain and could organize effective ambushes against superior enemy forces. They usually wore a shaggy felt hat and a tunic of coarse cloth, the basic dress of the Greek peasant or shepherd. Sometimes a makeshift shield, consisting of an animal pelt laid along the left arm and secured in place by knotting a pair of its paws around the neck, could be used by these skirmishers. The *psiloi* of the Macedonian Army were organized into large companies, with 500 men in each, but the total number of companies varied widely. In addition to these, the Macedonian infantry included some separate units of archers (*toxotai*). These consisted of three companies with 500 men each, assembled into a Corps of Archers that was under overall command of a single officer. The first company was formed by Cretans, while the other two were made up of Macedonian hunters. The Cretan archers were mercenaries contracted on a fixed basis by the Macedonian Army, the island of Crete being famous throughout the ancient world as the home of the best Greek archers. Cretan mercenaries were employed across the Mediterranean by several states, earning a strong military reputation thanks to their incredible skills.

Finally, the light infantry of the Macedonian Army comprised several allied contingents sent by the Paeonian, Illyrian and Thracian tribes that had been submitted by Philip II. These excellent skirmishers were not equipped like the *psiloi*, but carried the standard panoply of the peltasts (with throwing javelins and small shield). Despite being made up of foreigners who had only recently fought against Alexander, these Balkan tribal contingents performed extremely well in Asia and showed a high degree of loyalty. According to ancient sources, the best of these tribal light infantrymen were the Agrianes, who were part of the Paeonians. They were specialized in mountain warfare and could easily climb over any mountain or hill. These crack Agrianes peltasts came from the household troops of a tribal king who had accepted Macedonian suzerainty, and thus were chosen soldiers. Initially they were organized into a single company with 500 men, but the arrival of reinforcements from Paeonia permitted the creation of a second company, which had the same establishment as the existing one. In total, the Balkan communities provided some 7,000 tribal light infantrymen for Alexander, most of them sent by the Odrysians and the Triballi, two of the most important Thracian tribes. The Macedonians structured the various contingents sent by the client kings into companies of 500 men like the rest of their light infantry. Sometimes these units were commanded by their own tribal leaders, but in several cases they were given an experienced Macedonian officer. Like the Greeks and the archers, the peltasts provided by the Balkan tribes had a single overall commander.

Under Alexander, the horse companions retained the basic organization that had been given to them by his father. They were structured on eight squadrons known as *ilai*, each of which comprised 200 horsemen. The only exception to this rule was the elite *basilike ile* (Royal Squadron) or *agema* (Vanguard), which had 400 men who acted as the mounted bodyguard of the king. The Royal Squadron was under the direct command of Alexander and its members were all aristocrats from the leading noble families of Macedonia. The eight squadrons of the horse companions acted as an independent cavalry regiment. Each squadron was divided into two sections of 100 men each, except the *agema* that had four sections, with each section divided into two *tetrarchiai* of fifty horsemen. The *ilai* were recruited territorially from the various districts of Macedonia. Named after their commanders, they were occasionally grouped together into a larger formation of three or four squadrons (a hipparchy). From their first organization, the horse companions were equipped as heavy cavalry, with cuirasses and helmets, so they acted as 'shock' troops on the battlefield and were mostly tasked with conducting frontal charges. The Macedonian cavalry, however, were only one of the six components that made up Alexander's mounted troops, serving together with the Thessalian, Greek and Paeonian/Thracian cavalry, as well as the *prodromoi* (light cavalry) and mercenary cavalry.

Thessaly was the only region of Greece with large plains for the breeding of horses, and thus was the only area of the southern Balkans where local rulers could field large cavalry armies. Differently from the Macedonians, whose cavalry was by now heavily equipped, the Thessalians fielded sizeable contingents of excellent light horsemen armed with javelins. Indeed, the tactical combination of heavy horse companions and light Thessalian cavalry quickly became one of the tactical keys of Alexander's success. When Alexander crossed into Asia to attack the Persian Empire, the Macedonian Army included 1,800 elite Thessalian light cavalry, organized very similarly to the horse companions as they were structured on a regiment with eight *ilai*. One of these squadrons had an elite status and a larger establishment with 400 troops, like the Macedonian *agema*, whereas all the others had 200 men each. The Thessalian squadron was entirely recruited from Pharsalians, the best cavalrymen of Thessaly. The fact that the Thessalian cavalry was organized on eight *ilai* like the Macedonian horse companions was important symbolically, underlining the strong political links existing between Macedonia and Thessaly. The two states were governed by the same monarch but were administered as separate entities. The cavalry contingent

Macedonian archer, equipped with short bow and small round shield. (*Photo and copyright by Athenea Prómakhos*)

Thracian slinger wearing a zeira cloak. (*Photo and copyright by Ancient Thrace*)

sent by the League of Corinth was quite limited from a numerical point of view, comprising just 600 horsemen who were organized into three squadrons of 200 men each. Cavalry had never been an important component of Greek warfare, and thus the various *poleis* had just a few horsemen in their armies. The first squadron of allied Greek cavalry comprised Peloponnesian and Achaean horsemen, while the second was made up of soldiers from Phthiotis and Malis in central Greece, and the third was recruited from Locrian and Phocian cavalrymen. Since no city in Greece was able to form and maintain a squadron of its own cavalry, these three units were organized by assembling together the various contingents from different areas of Greece. During most of Alexander's campaigns in Asia, the three squadrons of Greek cavalry were employed together and formed an independent hipparchy. During the final phases of Alexander's conquests, a second hipparchy of allied cavalry was raised in Greece and sent to Asia to support the Macedonian Army. Like the existing one, this comprised three squadrons of 200 men each: the first was formed with Boeotians, the second with Acarnanians and Aetolians, and the third with Eleians. All the cavalry sent by the League of Corinth were heavily equipped like the Macedonian horse companions.

The Paeonians and Thracians, in addition to sending large numbers of excellent light infantry, contributed to Alexander's war efforts by providing three squadrons of light cavalry. One of these squadrons, commanded by a tribal prince, was sent by the Paeonians, whereas the other two were provided by the Odrysians. As previously mentioned, Philip II had annexed a good portion of southern Thrace to the Kingdom of Macedonia. Consequently, he could start recruiting an increasing number of Thracians for his army and used these soldiers from the newly conquered regions to organize a new category of light cavalrymen: the *prodromoi* or 'scouts'. While formally Macedonians, in reality they were Thracians who had only recently been subdued by the Kingdom of Macedonia. The *prodromoi* had a very important tactical role, since they were equipped with throwing javelins and were trained to fight from a distance as mounted skirmishers. In total they comprised 800 men, organized into four squadrons of 200 men each. Their officers were all 'true' Macedonians. The *prodromoi* had the same combat capabilities as the Paeonian and Odrysian cavalry, but they were much more disciplined.

By the time Alexander became king, the use of mercenaries was very common in Greece, with the traditional way of warfare based on the primary role played by the citizen hoplites in decay. Many Greek cities preferred using mercenaries instead of raising their own contingents of hoplites. Additionally, several regions of Greece (the poorest ones) had progressively become specialized in providing mercenary contingents to the Persian Empire. The Persians, who lived a terrible period of civil wars after their failed Greek campaigns, admired the military capabilities of the

Macedonian horse companion in everyday dress, without cuirass and helmet. He is armed with a xysthon cavalry spear. (*Photo and copyright by Hetairoi*)

Macedonian horse companion wearing the national headgear of his kingdom, the kausia soft cap. (*Photo and copyright by Hetairoi*)

Greek hoplites and their superior combat tactics. As a result, thousands of Greek mercenaries were recruited by the Achaemenids and were included in the Persian Army (such as the famous 'Ten Thousand' commanded by Xenophon). Consequently, during his invasion of Asia Minor, Alexander faced a large contingent of Greek mercenary infantry that served under Persian flags. It is important to understand that the Greek mercenary cavalry employed by the Macedonians was entirely composed of light horsemen. Initially, the Macedonian Army included just a single squadron of mercenary cavalry, which was later left to help garrison Anatolia and thus played no part in the following military operations. As the hostilities progressed, however, Alexander realized he needed more light cavalry troops: as a result, two hipparchies of mercenary Greek cavalry, with two squadrons each, were raised before the decisive Battle of Gaugamela. Later, when the Macedonian Army reached the city of Ecbatana, the squadrons of allied Greek cavalry were disbanded. However, their members were encouraged to continue serving under Alexander by entering the ranks of the Greek mercenary cavalry. With the inclusion of these new men, the mercenary cavalry were expanded from two to three hipparchies. At the beginning of his campaigns in Asia, Alexander considered the mercenary cavalry to be expendable troops of low quality, but over time he started to appreciate the military capabilities of these professionals. Indeed, the mercenary horsemen had the same standards as Alexander's other light cavalry contingents.

After the Battle of Gaugamela, Alexander partially reformed the organization of the Macedonian Army in order to face his new military requirements. After receiving significant reinforcements from Macedonia, he increased the number of heavy infantry regiments from six to seven by creating a new one. In addition, Alexander started to recruit troops from his new subjects in Asia. By the time of his death, he had been able to raise and train a large body of 30,000 young Persians, who were known as *epigoni* or 'emulators'. This term derived from the fact that these new soldiers were trained and equipped like Macedonian phalangites. After Gaugamela, the Macedonian Army also started to include some units of Asian light cavalry, recruited from the warlike peoples living in the eastern provinces of the Persian Empire. These troops, generally armed with javelins, were called *hippakontistai*. The *epigoni* did not have the opportunity to be employed in battle before their disbandment, which took place shortly after Alexander's sudden death. However, the *hippakontistai* followed the Macedonian Army in the bloody campaign that it fought in India and played a prominent role at the Battle of the Hydaspes.

During Alexander's last military campaign in India, the elite Regiment of the Royal Hypaspists received silver-plated shields in reward for the excellent military services performed during several years of campaigning in Asia. As a result, the unit changed its name to the *Argyraspides* or 'silver shields'. Since 331 BC, the corps had been reorganized on three battalions with 1,000 men each, which were known as chiliarchies. The adoption of silver shields by the *Argyraspides* initiated a military tradition that continued during the Hellenistic period, which saw the formation of several elite infantry units having golden or silver shields across the kingdoms that emerged from the collapse of Alexander's empire.

Thessalian cavalry officer with petasos sun hat. (*Photo and copyright by Athenea Prómakhos*)

Thessalian light cavalryman with krepides boots. (*Photo and copyright by Hetairoi*)

Chapter 4

The Conquest of the Persian Empire

After assembling his forces, Alexander crossed the Hellespont at the head of the Macedonian Army in 334 BC. More than 100 triremes were needed to transport his 37,000 soldiers to Asia Minor. This was an impressive size for an army for the Greek standards of the time, especially considering that most of these soldiers were battle-hardened veterans with previous combat experience. However, compared to the vast forces available to the Persians, Alexander's military resources appeared puny. The Persian Empire was the greatest state of the ancient world, covering an immense amount of territory that stretched from Asia Minor in the west to India in the east, and from central Asia in the north to Egypt in the south. The Achaemenids had been able to absorb into their expanding state some of the most important civilizations of Antiquity. For example, the Persians were culturally the direct heirs of the Babylonians and the Assyrians. It should be remembered, however, that they were of nomadic origin and that their homeland was in the heart of present-day Iran, not in Mesopotamia. The Persians had begun their conquests with another warlike Iranian people, the Medes. However, at some point the Medes had tried to assume control over the empire that they were building with the Persians, so an internal conflict broke out between them. The Persians eventually prevailed, imposing themselves over their former allies. The Achaemenid Empire was inhabited by millions of people and comprised dozens of countries; consequently, its military resources were vast. The individual Persian territories were organized as autonomous provinces or satrapies, each of which had its own governor, but the central government of the Achaemenids was able to exert direct control over the provinces thanks to an effective network of roads and a solid administrative system. The scope of the Persians' military resources is illustrated by the fact that each of the satrapies was able to deploy an army of at least 30,000 men, so Alexander's forces had the same numerical consistency as a single Persian provincial army.

The Achaemenid forces comprised a myriad of different troop types, since all the peoples living inside the Persian Empire sent large contingents of warriors, who were equipped and fought according to the military traditions of their home communities. As a result, many different kinds of combat specialization could be found inside the Persian Army. Nevertheless, the Achaemenid forces had two structural weaknesses.

First of all, the armies were not permanent like the Macedonian ones: the Persian troops were mobilized only in case of necessity and did not serve in time of peace. The only exception to this rule were the famous Immortals, the imperial guard of the Achaemenid rulers, who comprised a total of 10,000 chosen soldiers. The Immortals were always on active service and could be employed at any time. The other Persian military forces, however, were only assembled into temporary divisions when needed. The second weak point of the Achaemenid military apparatus was the general lack of heavy infantry troops. All the peoples living inside the Persian Empire were used to equipping their foot warriors as light skirmishers armed with only javelins or bows. As a result, the Achaemenids had no heavy infantry that could fight against the heavily armoured Greek hoplites on equal terms. They tried to resolve this problem by recruiting increasing numbers of Hellenic mercenaries, but their loyalty was always subordinate to the regularity of their payments. Consequently, from a tactical point of view, a single Macedonian phalangite corresponded to at least ten Persian skirmishers on the field of battle, so the massive numerical superiority of the Achaemenids was greatly reduced by the qualitative superiority of Alexander's troops. The Persians did, however, have a large and effective navy that was clearly superior to that employed by the Macedonians. The Persians could have attacked Alexander's ships during their crossing of the Hellespont, but instead preferred avoiding direct confrontation. This was the greatest strategic mistake made by the Achaemenids in their war against Alexander, but it should be borne in mind that the terrible memories of the Battle of Salamis were still fresh in Persia.

Darius III, the supreme ruler of the Achaemenid Empire, did not consider Alexander and his Macedonians as a serious military threat. He was convinced that the invaders would never be able to advance deeply into Asia Minor, and had a very poor opinion of the Macedonian king. Memnon of Rhodes, the commander of the Greek mercenaries serving in the Persian Army and one of Darius' main military advisors, suggested avoiding a direct confrontation with the Macedonians, inviting his Persian employers to adopt a prudent but effective scorched earth strategy. By destroying all the food resources of Asia Minor before the invaders could take control of them, the Persians would have caused a terrible logistical crisis for the Macedonian Army that would have obliged Alexander to abandon his invasion before it really got started. Memnon's suggested strategy was a wise one, since the invaders would have soon found themselves with a lengthy supply line stretching across Anatolia. Once far from their bases on the coast of Asia Minor, the Macedonians would have been obliged to rely on local food resources and their supply lines would have been dangerously exposed to attacks by the Persian skirmishers. Memnon's strategic advice, however, was rejected by Darius and his Persian generals. Darius was unwilling to

Thessalian light cavalryman with crescent-shaped pelte shield. (*Photo and copyright by Athenea Prómakhos*)

Detail of a Thessalian petasos sun hat made of wicker. (*Photo and copyright by Hetairoi*)

destroy the economy of his western satrapies just because a bold but inexperienced foreign king had landed in Asia. As a result, the Persians decided to mobilize the forces of their five Anatolian provinces and send them against Alexander as soon as possible to halt his advance.

The Macedonians clashed with the Anatolian satraps at the Battle of the Granicus River in May 334 BC, not far from the Hellespont. The army mobilized by the Persians for this first clash with Alexander was not a large one, comprising just 40,000 men, so the Macedonians were not overwhelmed numerically. Between the two opposing armies was the Granicus River, which the Persians tried to use to their advantage: instead of attacking the enemy, they waited for Alexander to move. To crush the Persian army, the Macedonians would be obliged to cross the river under the arrows of the Persians and leave themselves open to a sudden counter-attack. Alexander deployed his troops in a way that would become distinctive of his tactics: phalangites in the middle, heavy cavalry on the right wing and light cavalry on the left wing. The Macedonian king was in command of the horse companions, who were tasked with launching the attack against the Persian left. The clash began with a feint of the Macedonian left, which attacked the Persians to attract their attention. The Achaemenids took the bait and sent significant reinforcements against Alexander's light cavalry. At this point, seeing that the Persian left wing had been weakened, Alexander launched the charge of his horse companions. Deployed in their wedge formation, they crossed the Granicus with no hesitation and smashed into the Persian centre, killing a great number of enemy infantry. The Achaemenids responded by organizing a counter-attack with their best cavalry, and during the ensuing melee between mounted troops the young king was wounded by a Persian who attacked him from the rear. One of Alexander's friends, Cleitus, severed the outstretched arm of the enemy cavalryman who was trying to kill Alexander, thus saving the life of his king. After some harsh fighting on the muddy banks of the Granicus, the horse companions prevailed over the Persian cavalry thanks to their long spears (the Achaemenid horsemen were armed only with javelins, which were of little use in close combat) and the direct support given by the hypaspists. After opening a huge hole in the Persian formations, Alexander ordered a general advance of his phalanxes while attacking the Persian infantry with his heavy cavalry. The foot companions thus crossed the Granicus without encountering any opposition and attacked the Persian infantry from the rear. Alexander continued his advance and attacked the rear of the Persian cavalry that was fighting against his own light mounted troops. The attack of the phalangites sealed victory for Alexander, routing the Persian forces and obliging them to fall back in disorder.

The Battle of the Granicus River was a great success for Alexander, with some 14,000 Persians killed or captured against just 400 Macedonian casualties. The Persian army at the Granicus River also included 18,000 elite Greek mercenaries under Memnon of Rhodes, who acted as the overall Achaemenid commander during the battle. These men were kept in reserve during the clash, but were abandoned by the fleeing Persians. Surrounded by Alexander's cavalry, the Greek infantry were massacred: 10,000 of them were killed and the remaining 8,000 were captured by the Macedonians, who enslaved them and sent them back to Greece to work in Alexander's mines. Memnon, however, escaped. After destroying the forces of the Anatolian satrapies, the Macedonians freed all the Greek cities of Asia Minor that had long been under Persian rule. Alexander was welcomed as a liberator by all the *poleis* of western Anatolia, which were granted the right of establishing forms of self-government based on democratic principles. Against all expectations, Alexander did not impose a strict rule over the lands that he conquered, with all the Persian satraps who surrendered to him without fighting being permitted to retain their administrative functions while the populations could continue living according to their traditions. No attempts were made to impose Hellenic customs, and taxes were collected in a fair way. Alexander thereby prevented the outbreak of revolts in his newly conquered lands by respecting the traditions and rights of the local peoples. After acquiring control over most of the Anatolian strongholds without fighting, the Macedonians moved to the very south of Asia Minor to besiege the only fortified city that was still in Persian hands: Halicarnassus. This was an important naval base for

Thracian, Thracian/Phrygian and Phrygian helmets (from left to right). (*Photo and copyright by Hetairoi*)

the Achaemenids and was garrisoned by a sizeable number of troops under command of Memnon. After a brief but violent siege, the Macedonians opened a breech in the walls of Halicarnassus and stormed the city. Recognizing the futility of further resistance, Memnon abandoned his positions and ordered his retreating soldiers to burn Halicarnassus. Soon after these events, Memnon was killed while besieging Mytilene as he tried to instigate a revolt against Alexander's rule in Asia Minot.

After obtaining control of Halicarnassus, Alexander could continue his march southwards and crossed the region of Cappadocia unopposed. To enter the rich Persian territories of Syria from the north he had to cross the narrow passes of the Taurus Mountains, commonly known as the 'Cilician Gates'. These could have been easily defended by the local Persian forces, but the Cappadocian satrap wanted to avoid any direct confrontation with Alexander. As a result, the Macedonians entered northern Syria unopposed. While these events took place around the Taurus Mountains, Darius, finally starting to consider Alexander as a serious menace for the stability of his empire, had begun assembling a large army in the heart of his richest provinces. The Macedonians would now have to face the best soldiers of the Persian Army, including the 10,000 Immortals. Darius advanced at the head of some 100,000 soldiers in a bid to eject the invaders. The Persians did not attack

Three different versions of Attic helmet used by the Macedonian Army. (*Photo and copyright by Hetairoi*)

the Macedonians directly, but advanced from the east against their supply lines that stretched across the Taurus Mountains. Alexander was forced to march back to intercept Darius before he could cut his lines of supply running between southern Anatolia and northern Syria.

The two armies clashed at Issus, on the coastline connecting Anatolia with Syria and near the mouth of the Pinarus River. The Macedonians were at a clear numerical disadvantage, but Alexander was not overawed by the superiority of the Persians. He deployed his forces in the usual way: light cavalry on the left (near the mouth of the Pinarus), phalanxes in the centre and heavy cavalry on the right. Darius concentrated all his cavalry on his right near the mouth of the Pinarus. The Persians also deployed a substantial number of Greek mercenaries, some 12,000 in total, who were stationed in the centre of their line. The Achaemenids attacked first with their cavalry, which comprised a large number of heavily armoured cataphracts, investing the light cavalry of the Macedonian left that mostly consisted of Thessalians. Alexander responded by crossing the Pinarus at the head of his horse companions and ordering a general advance of his infantry in the centre. This time the Macedonian infantry had some difficulties in crossing in front of the enemy, since they were opposed by Greek mercenaries. Soon, however, the hypaspists were able to punch a hole through the Persian left wing. At this point, Alexander and his heavy cavalry launched a charge against the Persian centre and advanced against Darius with the clear intention of

Detail of three different versions of Attic helmet used by the Macedonian Army. (*Photo and copyright by Hetairoi*)

killing him. The Persian infantry was routed and suffered severe losses, since its best elements (the Greek mercenaries) were already fighting against the phalangites and could not help Darius. The Persian king, fearing for his life, abandoned the battlefield before his army collapsed. Alexander then surrounded and attacked the Greek mercenaries, who were still resisting the advance of the phalangites; these professional soldiers, like those of Memnon at the Granicus, did not surrender and thus suffered heavy losses. By the end of the battle, 30,000 Persians had been killed,

Boeotian, Pilos and Attic-Boeotian helmets (from left to right). (*Photo and copyright by Hetairoi*)

while the Macedonians suffered just 450 casualties. Alexander captured Darius' wife and daughters soon after the clash and was now free to occupy the rich regions of the Middle East. The pride of the Persian Army had been crushed and the reputation of Darius as a military commander had been seriously damaged. After the Battle of Issus, the Achaemenid ruler tried to find a compromise with Alexander, having also lost part of his imperial treasure during the ensuing rout. Darius proposed a partition of the Persian territories with Alexander: the Achaemenids would retain the eastern satrapies of the empire, with the Macedonians controlling those in the west. Alexander rejected Darius' proposal and continued his advance across Syria, one of the richest regions of the Persian Empire, which he rapidly conquered.

Moving south, the Macedonian Army occupied Phoenicia. Corresponding to present-day Lebanon, this region was of great strategic significance for the Achaemenids since it was there that the Persian Navy had its most important bases and arsenals. The coastal city of Tyre, in particular, was the key military location in Phoenicia, the last major port of the Persians on the Mediterranean that had not yet been conquered by the Macedonians. Alexander understood that if he occupied Tyre, the Persian Navy would soon run out of supplies. Until that moment, both sides had avoided a major naval battle, although for different reasons: the Macedonians did not have a very high opinion of the Greek sailors who made up the crews of their fleet, whereas the Achaemenids feared the technological superiority of the enemy's warships. Consequently, both navies remained inactive during the early phase of Alexander's invasion. However, the Persians had lost all their other ports since Alexander had followed a coastal route during his advances. Now he had the

Boeotian, Attic-Boeotian and Attic helmets (from left to right). (*Photo and copyright by Hetairoi*)

Detail of Attic, Attic-Boeotian and Boeotian helmets (from left to right). (*Photo and copyright by Hetairoi*)

opportunity to besiege Tyre and eliminate forever the menace represented by the Persian Navy. The fortifications of Tyre were extremely strong. The city was enclosed by massive walls and was connected to a nearby island that had two natural harbours on the landward side. After trying to find a compromise with the Tyrians by promising to respect their commercial interests, Alexander had no choice but to began the siege of the Phoenician city in 332 BC. Since the Macedonians could not attack Tyre from the sea and the external walls of the city were too strong to be breached, Alexander ordered the construction of a kilometre-long causeway that stretched out to the island in front of Tyre. Such an audacious project of military engineering seemed impossible, but the Macedonians were nevertheless able to build the causeway, which was used to move two massive siege towers (150ft high) to the island. The Tyrians, seeing the danger posed by Alexander's plans, mounted a counter-attack. They took an old transport ship and filled it with dried branches, pitch, sulphur and other combustibles, then set fire to the ship and ran it up against the causeway built by the Macedonians. The attack was a success, destroying the two siege towers. Alexander now realized that he would never conquer Tyre without a navy. Since his Greek ships were still in the Hellespont transporting supplies, he assembled a new fleet by using the naval contingents of the recently conquered cities of Asia Minor. These consisted of eighty warships, which were augmented to 200 when the island of Cyprus sent another 120 vessels. While formally part of the Persian Empire, the cities of Cyprus had always enjoyed a high degree of autonomy. After the Battle of Issus, seeing that the Macedonians were on the verge of completing their conquest of Phoenicia, the various cities of Cyprus (whose populations were mostly Greek) decided to support Alexander by sending him their fleets. With a naval squadron of 200 vessels, Alexander could now blockade both ports of Tyre and prevent the arrival of supplies by sea for the besieged Phoenicians. The Macedonians then mounted battering rams on their warships and started to attack the fortifications of the island, trying to open a breach in the walls. When this succeeded, Alexander ordered a massive assault and bombardment. Although the defenders of Tyre put up a desperate resistance, they were eventually all massacred. Half of the city was destroyed and 30,000 of its inhabitants were captured to be sold as slaves.

With the conquest of Tyre, the Persian Navy lost its last base and ceased to be a menace for the Macedonians. Alexander's next target was Egypt, one of the richest lands of the ancient world. Egypt had been conquered by the Persians shortly before their ill-fated Greek expeditions and had always been the most troublesome of the Achaemenid provinces. Indeed, the Egyptians never accepted Persian suzerainty, being proud of their glorious traditions. During the two centuries of Achaemenid rule, Egypt revolted against the Persians on several occasions and was able to regain independence for brief periods. As a consequence, Alexander was sure that the Egyptians would join his cause with great enthusiasm and that they would provide him with a number of their excellent warships. Before entering the 'Land of the Nile', however, the Macedonians had to overcome the resistance of one last Persian stronghold that was located in the south of Palestine: the fortified city of Gaza. The siege of Gaza, which was built on a hill, proved to be an extremely difficult one for Alexander, exactly like that of Tyre. The inhabitants of the city, together with their Nabatean allies, had no intention of surrendering, repulsing three assaults by the besiegers. The Macedonians suffered severe losses, and during one of their fruitless attacks Alexander was seriously wounded by an enemy arrow. Nevertheless, the Macedonians were eventually able to storm Gaza and crush the resistance of the defenders. All the male inhabitants of the city were killed, while the women and children were sold into slavery. After the conquest of the city, Alexander could finally enter Egypt, where he was welcomed as a liberator by the local population and was made pharaoh. The Macedonians were surprised by the incredible enthusiasm of the Egyptians, who considered Alexander to be the reincarnation of their gods Ra and Osiris. The Macedonian king showed great respect for Egyptian culture and religion, left the administration of the country in the hands of the local ruling classes and initiated the building of a new coastal city that was named Alexandria after himself. Such acts did nothing but augment the love of the Egyptians for Alexander, who could now count on massive amounts of grain and money from them.

While all these events took place in Asia and North Africa, the political and military situation in his European domains began to worsen for Alexander. Sparta, the only Greek city that had never fully accepted Macedonian suzerainty over the Hellenic world, had started working at the formation of a military alliance with the

Persian Empire. At that time the city was ruled by the ambitious Agis III, who was eager to restore Spartan hegemony in the Peloponnese by every method possible. In 333 BC, Agis sent an embassy to the Achaemenids asking for financial and naval support in order to initiate a conflict against the Macedonians in southern Greece. The Persians agreed to help Agis, but could send him only a small sum of money and ten warships since they were so heavily involved on other fronts. Despite this, the Spartan monarch continued to prepare his forces for a confrontation with the Macedonians. The Macedonians had small garrisons in all the most important cities of Greece, but their main army was fighting in Asia, so in the event of a full-scale Greek rebellion, the Macedonians would have experienced great difficulties in retaining control over the major *poleis*. Before starting his invasion of the Persian Empire, Alexander had nominated his experienced general Antipater as the regent of Macedonia. He had also ordered the formation of twelve new military units: eight regiments of infantry and four squadrons of cavalry. These would make up the military garrison of Macedonia and Greece during his long absence and be under the orders of Antipater. It should be noted, however, that these new military units were not comprised of veterans like those serving in Asia, and thus were not of the highest quality. The young king was well aware that not only the Greeks but also the Thracians could have revolted against his rule while he was away, so he appointed a separate governor for Thrace who acted independently from Antipater and had a force of 30,000 soldiers under his direct command. This man named by Alexander was Zopyrion, who was a very ambitious man, just like Antipater. In 331 BC, Zopyrion decided to launch a campaign against the Scythians in a bid to secure glory for himself while Alexander was conquering Asia. However, this expedition ended in disaster, becoming the worst defeat ever suffered by the Macedonian Army. During their ill-fated invasion of Scythian lands, Zopyrion's 30,000 men were all killed. According to primary sources, the Macedonian forces operating in the eastern Balkans were not defeated in a pitched battle but during a series of raids that were launched by the Scythians. After achieving very little, Zopyrion abandoned Scythian lands that he had conquered and marched back south, but during the retreat his forces were constantly harassed by the Scythians and were also ambushed by the Thracian tribes of the Getae and Triballi which revolted against Macedonia.

The defeat and death of Zopyrion shocked Antipater, who now had to quell the rebellion of the Thracians while still keeping an eye on the Greeks with only a limited number of troops. After learning of the Macedonians' terrible defeat in Scythia and the outbreak of revolts in Thrace, Agis III decided to act, declaring war on Macedonia and employing 8,000 Greek mercenaries who had previously served in the Persian Army, some whom were survivors of Issus. The Spartan king was able to assemble

Thracian/Phrygian helmet. (*Photo and copyright by Hetairoi*)

Thracian helmet. (*Photo and copyright by Hetairoi*)

a large force with 20,000 infantry and 2,000 cavalry, which included some Cretan mercenary archers and hoplites sent by Sparta's allies in the Peloponnese. In response, Antipater sent part of his army, under the command of a general named Coragus, against the Spartans, but they were defeated in battle. The regent of Macedonia was left with no option but to intervene personally with all his remaining troops against Agis. The Spartan monarch's army had been strengthened by the addition of many Greeks from Achaea and Arcadia. The decisive clash of this little-known war took place outside the city of Megalopolis, which had been besieged by the Spartans since it remained loyal to Macedonia. Antipater reached Megalopolis while it was still under siege and engaged Agis in battle. The Spartans were utterly defeated, with over 5,000 men and their king being killed. After restoring the status quo in Greece, Antipater turned his attention to Thrace and quelled the rebellion of the tribes there by employing very harsh methods. With order reimposed, he left a military garrison in the region that comprised just 4,000 foot soldiers and 2,000 cavalry. Not long before his death, Alexander appointed a new governor for Thrace: the talented and experienced military commander Lysimachus. Soon after his arrival in Thrace, the Odrysians and various other client communities revolted against the Macedonians in the hope of regaining their independence. This Thracian rebellion was particularly violent, and Lysimachus experienced many difficulties in crushing it. He was vastly outnumbered by the Thracians and was forced to fight a major pitched battle when it appeared he had little hope of success. However, the clash ended in victory for the Macedonians, despite significant losses suffered by Lysimachus' troops. By 320 BC, the Macedonian general had secured control over Thrace and could rule the region as one of the several independent kingdoms that were created after the collapse of Alexander's vast empire.

In 331 BC, after having completed the conquest of Egypt and the whole Mediterranean coastline of the Persian Empire, Alexander briefly reorganized his forces in preparation for the most decisive of his battles. Until that moment, the Macedonians had advanced along the coast in order to capture all the naval bases of the enemy fleet. This strategy had worked well, and Alexander could now exert total control over the eastern part of the Mediterranean. At this point of his invasion of Asia, however, Alexander had to move into the interior of the Achaemenid-held territories and face the bulk of the Persian forces. The Battle of Issus had been a brilliant victory, but only 100,000 enemy soldiers had taken part in it: the massive military resources of Darius III were still almost intact and thus the pivotal clash of the war was yet to come. The location for this crucial battle would be Mesopotamia, probably the richest region of Antiquity, where the first civilizations of history had emerged several centuries before. Mesopotamia – the 'land between the two rivers'

Macedonian foot companion wearing a magnificent example of Phrygian helmet. (*Photo and copyright by Hetairoi*)

Attic helmet. (*Photo and copyright by Hetairoi*)

– was extremely fertile as it was crossed by the Tigris and Euphrates. These rivers were the two most important waterways of the Middle East, so controlling their course was fundamental strategically. Mesopotamia, together with present-day Iran, was the very heart of the Persian Empire. One of the empire's four capitals, Babylon, was located there, together with several other large cities. Darius, who understood that if he was to lose Mesopotamia it would have been impossible for him to save his empire, started to mobilize his full military potential for a massive pitched battle to decide his destiny. Mesopotamia is a flat region entirely covered by vast plains, so the upcoming battle would be fought in favourable conditions for the Persians, who would be able to deploy their numerical superiority. When the Macedonians resumed their advance east from Syria, Darius could have stopped them during the crossing of the Tigris and of the Euphrates, which represented formidable natural barriers. However, he did not attempt to attack Alexander while he was advancing, preferring to remain further east in order to complete the mobilization of his forces. The Persians had already fought two pitched battles with a river between them and their enemy, and both had ended in disaster. Darius wanted to restore Persia's military reputation by defeating the invaders on the open field. He was confident that sheer numbers would defeat Alexander, mobilizing all the soldiers that were at his disposal, from every province of the Achaemenid Empire.

After crossing the Euphrates, the Macedonians followed a northern route instead of advancing on Babylon to the south-east. Alexander wanted to crush Darius before seizing the capital of Mesopotamia. After a short march, the Macedonians also crossed the Tigris in order to catch up with Darius, who was with his army on the eastern bank of the great river. The opposing armies clashed at Gaugamela, present-day Tel Gomel in the region of Kurdistan. When the Macedonians reached Gaugamela, their morale was very high, as several days before there had been a lunar eclipse that was interpreted as a positive omen for the destiny of Alexander. This time, however, Darius had chosen the battlefield well. Gaugamela consisted of a vast plain, with terrain that was flattened by the Persians before the arrival of the Macedonians. The Achaemenid monarch had been able to assemble an immense army, with 150,000 warriors coming from every corner of his realm: 10,000 Immortals, 10,000 Greek mercenaries, 90,000 other infantry and 40,000 cavalry. In addition, Darius could count on three special troop types whose tactics he hoped would decide the outcome of the battle: 2,000 heavily armoured cataphracts from Bactria, 200 scythed chariots and fifteen war elephants from India. The Persians' intentions were clear: they wanted to launch a massive frontal charge on the flattened terrain with these 'shock' troops in order to crush Alexander's phalanxes. The Macedonians had never before faced scythed chariots or war elephants, and Darius predicted they would thus not be able to stop the Persian attack. The war chariots had scythe blades mounted on their wheels which could cut dozens of men into pieces, while the war elephants were enormous beasts that it was felt would instil panic in the Macedonians.

Scythed chariots had already been employed by the Persians on several occasions, and had always caused serious losses to their enemies, proving very effective when used against foot troops. Each chariot had two blades, around a metre long, mounted on its two wheels, was pulled by a team of four horses and was manned by a crew of three men: one driver and two warriors. The main tactical task of the war chariots was to plough through lines of enemy infantry, cutting soldiers in half and opening huge gaps in the opposition lines that could be exploited by the cavalry. During previous battles, the Persians had seen that it was practically impossible to get horses to charge into the tight phalanxes of the Macedonians, which formed a wall of pikes when deployed in defensive formation. This problem, however, could be solved by using war chariots, since these could break the lines of the phalangites with their deadly blades. The tactical function of the war elephants was similar to that of the scythed chariots: to destroy everything they encountered, breaking the Macedonian pikes with their massive bodies (that were protected by armour) and trampling on the enemy foot soldiers. The 2,000 Persian cataphracts came from the border region of Bactria, which was located in Central Asia and whose governor was the

Attic-Boeotian helmet. (*Photo and copyright by Hetairoi*)

ambitious Bessus, an experienced military commander and the most powerful of the eastern satraps. The Bactrian cataphracts were equipped exactly like their Scythian equivalents, who had fought against the Persians in the steppes. They were fully armoured, with their horses also wearing massive scale-armour. In addition, they were armed with long and heavy spears that had to be used with both hands. Unlike the great majority of the Persian cavalry, the cataphracts were heavily enough equipped to face the Macedonian horse companions on almost equal terms. Furthermore, they were trained to operate with the war chariots in order to charge across the gaps that they opened.

To face Darius' 150,000 troops, Alexander's Macedonians comprised 47,000 men: 31,000 heavy infantry, 9,000 light infantry and 7,000 horsemen. The Persians deployed

Attic, Chalcidian, Attic and Chalcidian helmets (from left to right). (*Photo and copyright by Athenea Prómakhos*)

their forces with the war chariots to the front, the infantry in the centre and the cavalry on the two wings. Shortly before the start of the clash, being overconfident about the capabilities of his charioteers, Darius decided to deploy the 15 war elephants at the rear of his army as a strategic reserve guarding the Persian camp. This was a grave mistake, since the sight of the Indian beasts could have shocked the Macedonians psychologically, giving a great advantage to Darius' troops.

The Macedonian line, having the same composition as Alexander's previous battles, was surpassed by the longer Persian one by over a mile, so it seemed inevitable that his army would be outflanked by the Achaemenid troops. As a result, Alexander decided to assemble part of his heavy infantry (not the elite Macedonian *taxeis*) at the back of his forces in order to have a mobile reserve that could counter any outflanking manoeuvre by the enemy. The Battle of Gaugamela began with a general advance of the phalanxes against the centre of the Persian host, to which Darius responded by sending most of his cavalry against the left wing of the Macedonians. Instead of supporting the phalanxes or sending reinforcements to his left wing, Alexander took command of the horse companions and started to ride all the way to the edge of the Persian left wing that was located opposite him. This wing was mostly made up of heavy cavalry, comprising Bessus' Bactrian cataphracts as well as some contingents of Scythians who were allies of Darius. Understanding that Alexander had prevented him from attempting a flanking manoeuvre in that part of the battlefield, Darius ordered Bessus and his elite cavalry to charge against the Macedonian king. A furious cavalry battle broke out between the two mounted contingents, during which the Macedonians appeared at serious risk of being defeated and Alexander was in great danger. The Bactrians and Scythians fought with enormous courage. For the first time, the previously invincible horse companions experienced serious difficulties in defeating an enemy cavalry force. In the end, though, thanks to the arrival of reinforcements in the shape of the *prodromoi* light cavalry, Alexander prevailed against Bessus. The defeated Persian cavalry abandoned the battlefield and were followed in close pursuit by the *prodromoi*, who killed many of them as they fled.

Seeing that his left wing had been destroyed and that the phalanxes were about to smash into his centre, Darius decided to launch his planned attack with the war chariots in order to decide the outcome of the battle before the horse companions could turn left and attack his numerous infantry from the rear. The massed Persian scythed chariots advanced rapidly and reached the Macedonian front line at full speed, ready to break the ranks of the phalanxes. Alexander, however, had already prepared his foot soldiers for such an attack and they were ready to respond. During the final few metres of their advance, the Persian charioteers came under an intense rain of missiles from the light infantrymen of the Agrianes, who had been deployed in front of the phalangites under the protection of their pikes. Many drivers of the chariots were killed by the javelins of the Macedonian light infantry, with the result that the Persians lost most of their initial coordination. At this point the foot companions opened up their ranks in order to create alleys through which the chariots could pass. At the end of these alleys, the hypaspists were waiting for the enemy charioteers. The elite Macedonian light infantrymen attacked individual chariots from the rear once they had slowed them down after breaking up their formations. It was then extremely easy for the infantry to massacre the Persian drivers and neutralize all the war chariots. Alexander's tactics had worked perfectly and Darius had lost his crack 'shock' troops without inflicting any casualties on the enemy.

Soon after the Persian attack was repulsed, Alexander invested the Achaemenid centre with his horse companions deployed in wedge formation. The Persian infantry were attacked on their left by the Macedonian cavalry, while the phalanxes (which had resumed their advance) smashed into them from the front. This was the crucial moment that brought Alexander victory: the Persian centre collapsed and he charged with the horse companions against the position occupied by Darius. The Persian king risked being killed or captured by the Macedonian cavalrymen, who came very near to his chariot. Fortunately for Darius, the horse companions were temporarily slowed down by the strong resistance of the Immortals and the Greek mercenary hoplites, who gave him time to flee from the battlefield. Alexander was ready to follow in close pursuit to capture the Persian king and kill his remaining soldiers who

Linen cuirass reinforced with brass scales on the sides. (*Photo and copyright by Hetairoi*)

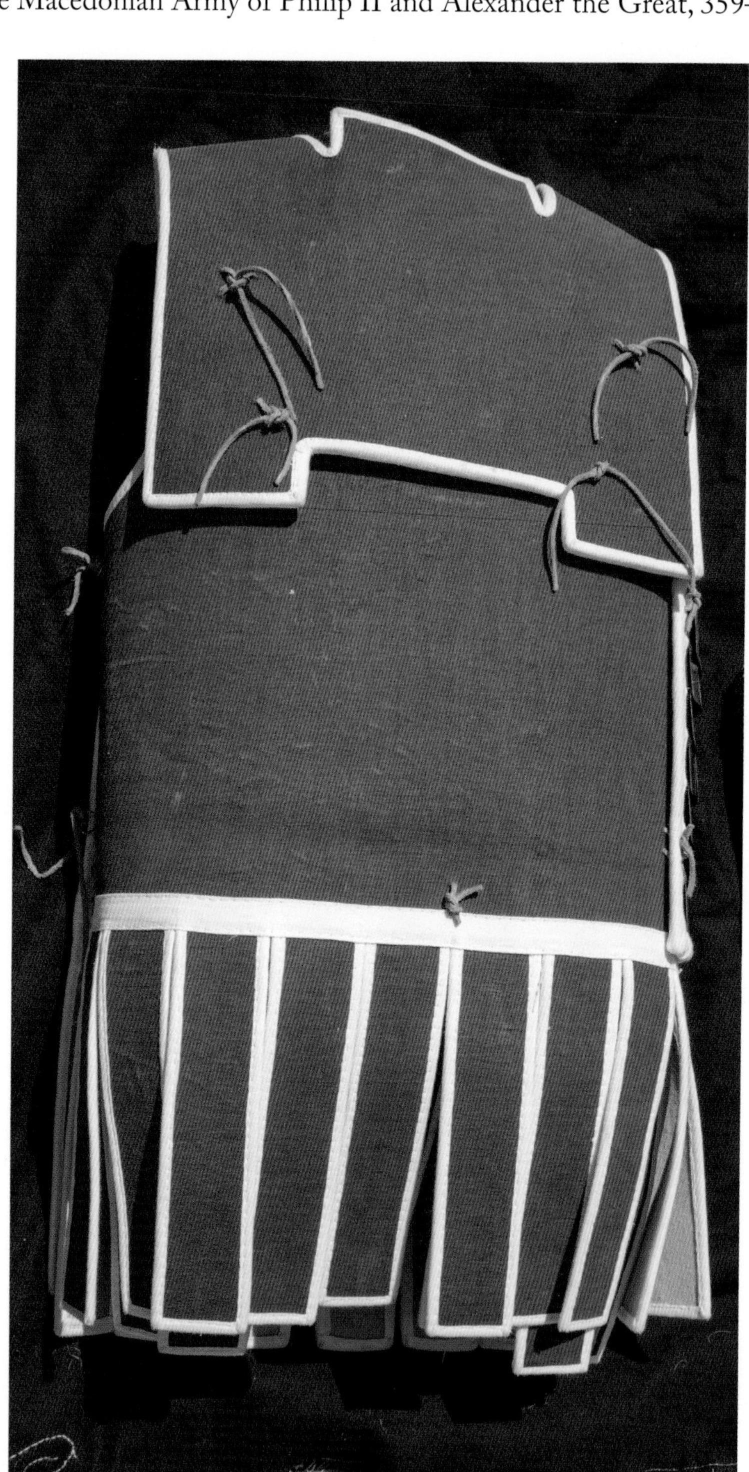

Detail of the back of a linen cuirass. (*Photo and copyright by Hetairoi*)

were falling back in complete disorder. At this point, however, he received a desperate request for help from his left wing, that was commanded by Parmenion. In that sector of the battlefield, the Persian cavalry had surrounded the Macedonians and was on the verge of destroying them. The Achaemenid mounted troops were much more numerous than the Macedonian light cavalry facing them, and thus the whole left wing of Alexander's army was running the risk of being crushed. Alexander had a very difficult decision to make: should he follow Darius and kill him in order to end the war, or should he return to the battlefield to save part of his army from destruction? In the end he decided to come back with his elite heavy cavalry and routed the Persian mounted troops that had surrounded Parmenion. In the aftermath of the battle, the Macedonians occupied the enemy camp, where they captured the Persian war elephants as well as Darius' baggage train that comprised vast amounts of gold. Gaugamela was a momentous triumph for Alexander, the Persians suffering a total of 50,000 casualties and losing all their best soldiers. Meanwhile, it was reported that the Macedonians lost only 1,500 men.

After defeating Darius on the battlefield for a second time, Alexander could invade southern Mesopotamia and occupy Babylon. The Macedonians entered the city in triumph and discovered a 'new world': Babylon, famous for its gardens and religious buildings, had been visited by only few Greek merchants prior to this time. The first of the four Persian capitals had fallen, and was soon followed by a second one, the magnificent city of Susa in Elam (on the eastern borders of modern Kuwait). Despite having been soundly defeated and having lost two of his richest cities, Darius still had no intention to surrender, as he continued to exert control over the eastern half of the Persian Empire, which comprised the heartland of his people (modern Iran) and several other provinces stretching south to India and north to Central Asia. All these lands were inhabited by warlike peoples, so Darius could easily recruit another army. In addition, some elite Achaemenid troops had been able to escape from the battlefield of Gaugamela and had followed their king: 1,000 Bactrian cataphracts commanded by Bessus, half of the Immortals and some 2,000 Greek mercenaries. Darius acted rapidly after this defeat, sending letters to all his eastern satraps ordering them to mobilize their forces. He also gave a speech in front of his remaining soldiers in order to boost their morale. The Achaemenid monarch then moved to Ecbatana, in the Zagros Mountains of Iran, where he started putting together a new army. To mobilize a sufficient number of troops and to organize them, however, Darius needed time. He therefore left behind 3,000 of his best remaining soldiers with orders to slow down Alexander's movements for as long as possible. These chosen troops were under the command of Ariobarzanes, one of the most experienced Persian generals.

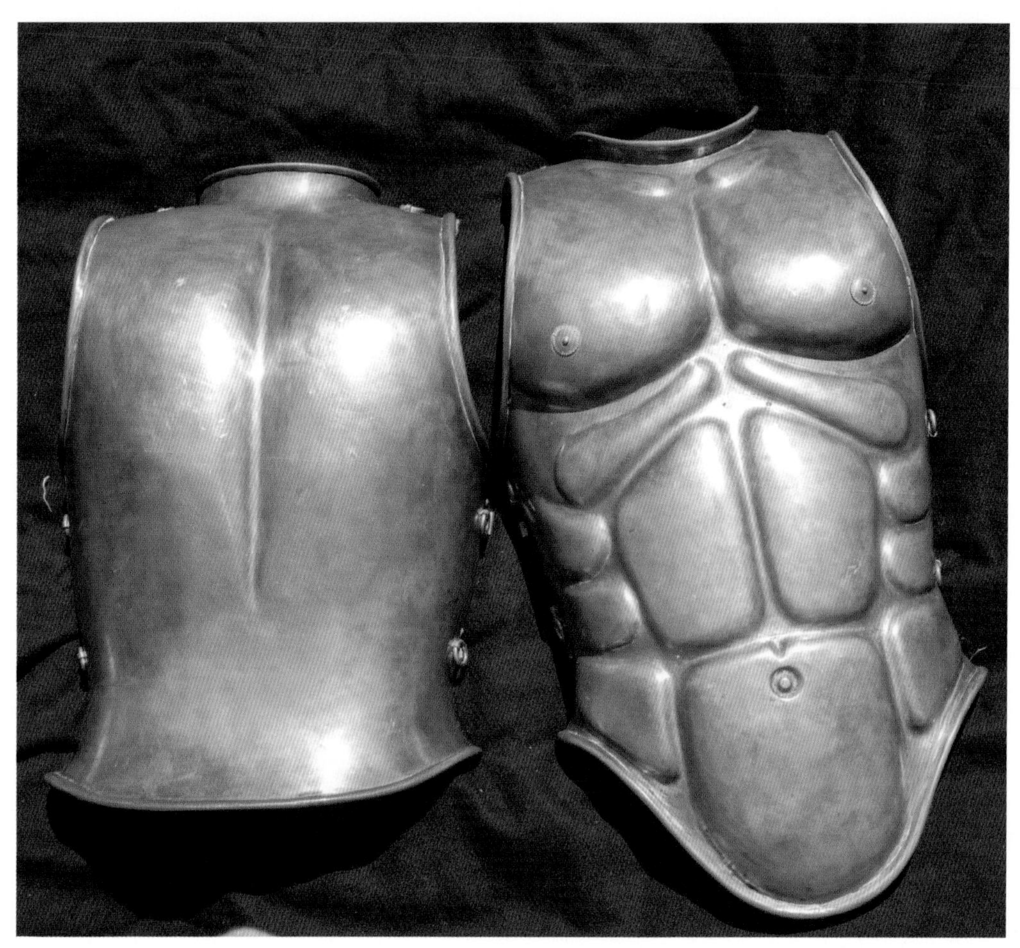

Detail of the back and front of a brass muscle cuirass. (*Photo and copyright by Hetairoi*)

To enter Iran, the Macedonians had no choice but to march on the Royal Road, a Persian 'highway' built several decades before by Darius I, which connected Susa with the two eastern capitals of the Achaemenids: Persepolis and Pasargadae. The terrain surrounding the Royal Road was covered by mountains, so marching across it during the winter months was a hazardous venture, especially for an army that did not have a great knowledge of the area. Only a few roads crossed the Zagros Mountains that marked the border between Mesopotamia and Persia, and these all passed through narrow mountain passes. Ariobarzanes had intimate knowledge of these passes and could have defended them for months with his few elite troops, providing Darius with the time he needed to raise his new army. After conquering Susa, Alexander continued his advance by dividing his army in two: one part, under command of Parmenion, moved along the Royal Road, while the other, under his own command, tried to cross the Zagros Mountains by traversing a narrow pass that

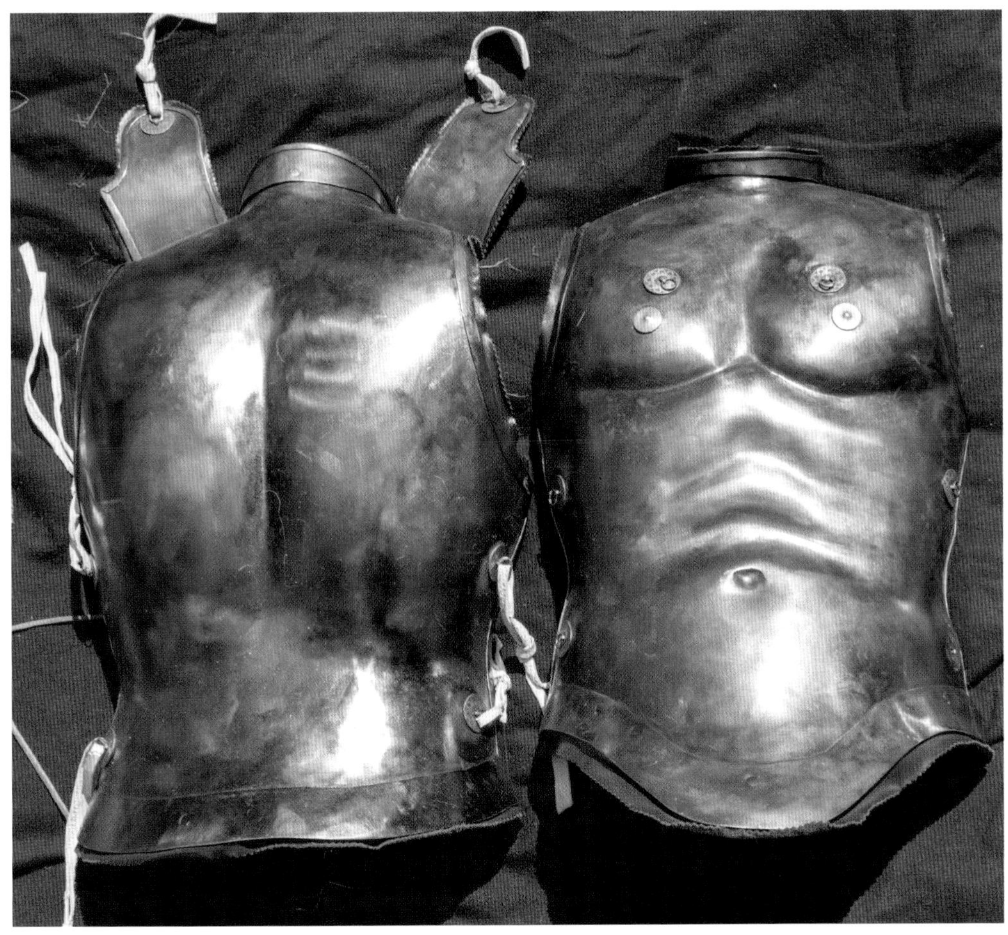

Detail of the back and front of a leather muscle cuirass. (*Photo and copyright by Hetairoi*)

was known as the Persian Gate. This pass was easy for a small number of men to defend, and was perfect for the staging of an ambush. During his advance, Alexander had to fight against local tribes such as the Uxians, who attacked him with hit-and-run tactics. Meanwhile, Ariobarzanes and his Persians prepared to mount a perfect ambush at the Persian Gate. The Persian Gate was preceded by a valley that was initially very wide, but progressively narrowed before reaching the mountain pass. Realizing that the Macedonians had poor knowledge of the terrain, the Persians deployed themselves on the slopes surrounding the Persian Gate and built a wall to block the pass, which at its narrowest point was just a couple of metres wide. Here, the Persians ambushed Alexander and his men, who probably numbered less than 10,000. Ariobarzanes' plan worked perfectly and the Macedonians suffered severe losses, the Achaemenid soldiers attacking them with a rain of arrows and boulders. Alexander had no choice but to fall back in order to reorganize his forces. During

Composite cuirass made of linen and reinforced with brass scales. (*Photo and copyright by Athenea Prómakhos*)

Examples of linen and composite cuirasses. (*Photo and copyright by Athenea Prómakhos*)

the following four weeks, the Persians defended the pass with great determination, like the Spartan hoplites had done at the pass of Thermopylae during the Second Persian War some 150 years previously. Ariobarzanes wanted to stop Alexander until the coming of spring, and possessed all the resources he needed to do so. Alexander, however, understood the risks that he was running in the heart of the mountains, and thus decided on a change of tactics. He organized a complex pincer attack, sending some of his best light infantry to climb over the hills that surrounded the Persian Gate. The defenders were taken by surprise, encircled and crushed after a harsh fight. Ariobarzanes had been confident that the Macedonians would be unable to find a path across the hills to attack his flanks, but it seems that Alexander employed some Persian prisoners as guides to show his troops the way. The Macedonians had conquered the Persian Gate, but at the cost of heavy casualties. Nevertheless, the defeat of Ariobarzanes removed the last military obstacle between Alexander and Persepolis, which was easily captured – as was Pasargadae – by the Macedonians, together with its treasury, which was considered to be the richest of the ancient world. Surprised by Alexander's victory at the Persian Gate, Darius had to abandon Ecbatana and move east in order to continue his mobilization.

Chapter 5

Alexander's Campaigns in Central Asia and India

After the Macedonians prevailed at the Persian Gate, Darius travelled to the eastern satrapies of Bactria and Sogdia, which were ruled by Bessus, the powerful governor. Bessus had commanded the left wing of the Persian army at Gaugamela, which was mostly made up of skilled warriors from his satrapies who were mobilized after the Battle of Issus. Bessus had been able to survive, together with part of his forces, the bloody clash at Gaugamela, and they had fled to Ecbatana with Darius. They now followed the king further east. Darius planned to raise a new army from the satrapies of Central Asia and gain time to prepare a counter-offensive against Alexander. With the end of winter, Alexander's troops again set off in pursuit of the Persians. They knew that only by capturing Darius could they finally bring the war to an end. While fleeing to Bactria, with the Macedonian cavalry in close pursuit, Bessus launched a conspiracy against Darius, together with the other satraps of the Central Asian provinces. Their plotting proved successful, and Darius was put in golden chains by the traitors, who hoped that by giving their king to Alexander they could obtain political advantage and retain their personal possessions. The most ambitious of them was Bessus, who wished to replace Darius as monarch and obtain control over the vast eastern provinces of the Achaemenid Empire. The rebel satraps tried to surrender Darius to the Macedonians, but Alexander would accept no agreement and ordered his men continue their pursuit of the remaining Persian forces. At this point, Bessus and the other plotters stabbed Darius and left him dying in a chariot that was found by the pursuing Macedonians. Thereafter, Bessus immediately proclaimed himself King of Persia, adopting the name Artaxerxes V. His self-proclaimed ascension to the throne could be seen as logical, since the Satrap of Bactria was the nearest noble to the monarch's heirs in the line of succession. When Alexander came upon Darius' body with his cavalry, he ordered them to bury the king with full honours and showed great respect for his former rival, promising that he would punish the regicides.

The death of Darius did not lead to the end of the war, which now continued between Alexander and Bessus. The Macedonians now began their conquest of Central Asia, which would finally lead them to India. In 329 BC, the Macedonians entered Bactria by way of the Hindu Kush mountain range, which Bessus had left undefended. Bessus had a simple plan: to move his forces ever further east, weakening the morale of the Macedonians and lengthening their supply lines. Having a superior knowledge of the terrain, he probably had in mind to conduct a guerrilla campaign against Alexander's army. Bessus intended to avoid any direct confrontations with the Macedonians but to cause continual losses to them with hit-and-run tactics and to burn crops while retreating, thereby wearing down Alexander's men. However, after crossing the Oxus River, which marks the modern border between Afghanistan and Tagikistan, the Bactrian mounted troops deserted and abandoned Bessus, who was seized by several of his chieftains and handed over to the pursuing Macedonians. He was then tortured and killed as punishment for having dethroned the legitimate monarch. With this move, Alexander won the support of numerous Persian nobles who were still loyal to the memory of Darius.

The death of Bessus, however, was not the end of Alexander's campaign in Central Asia: he had now conquered almost all the territories of the Persian Empire, but some of the border regions had not yet accepted his rule and continued to resist. Oxyartes, one of the satraps who had betrayed Bessus, became the new leader of the Persian resistance forces. Alexander resumed his advance north into the heart of Central Asia, capturing Samarkand (in modern Uzbekistan) and reaching the River Jaxartes, where he founded the city of Alexandria Eschate (Alexandria-the-Farthest). Despite these successes, the Macedonians had to face a number of uprisings from the indigenous Sogdian and Scythian tribesmen who remained loyal to Oxyartes. These mounted fighters of Central Asia employed their usual hit-and-run tactics against the Macedonians with great success, relying on their mastery of horsemanship and archery to attack the invaders from distance. During the interminable skirmishes fought against the Sogdians and Scythians, Alexander lost more soldiers than in any other of his campaigns. This started to generate discontent in the Macedonian Army, since Alexander's soldiers did not see the point of continuing their conquests in such an insignificant and poor region of the Persian Empire. The first rumblings of rebellion soon transformed into mutinies, forcing Alexander for the first time to face some of his army's internal problems. The Macedonian leaders had never faced guerrilla warfare before, and thus had to develop new tactics in order to defeat their nomadic enemies. These included combined use of catapults and archers to hit the enemy skirmishers operating on high ground, as well as carrying out costly sieges. The Sogdian mountain strongholds were formidable. Despite being injured on more than one occasion and suffering from dysentery, Alexander was finally able to win a decisive battle against the Scythians along the River Jaxartes.

With the defeat of the northern tribes, the Sogdians in the south decided to concentrate all their forces at a fortress called the Sogdian Rock, which was located

Front of a round pelte shield of the type used by the foot companions. (*Photo and copyright by Hetairoi*)

on top of a large escarpment. The fortress's name derived from the fact that it was considered impossible to conquer by all the inhabitants of the region. The actual site of the Sogdian Rock is still the subject of debate for historians, although the majority believe that it was probably located somewhere around Samarkand. Wherever its location, this defensive position of the Sogdians was incredibly strong. Soon after arriving at the fortress, Alexander worked out that the only way to take it was to use a picked group of elite soldiers, mountaineers who could climb with ropes and reach the top of the escarpment in order to launch a surprise attack on the garrison. Alexander called for volunteers, explaining to his troops the difficulties of their mission: to use ropes and tent-pegs in a night-time ascent. Some 300 men came forward to take part. Oxyartes had previously sent his wife and daughters to take refuge in the

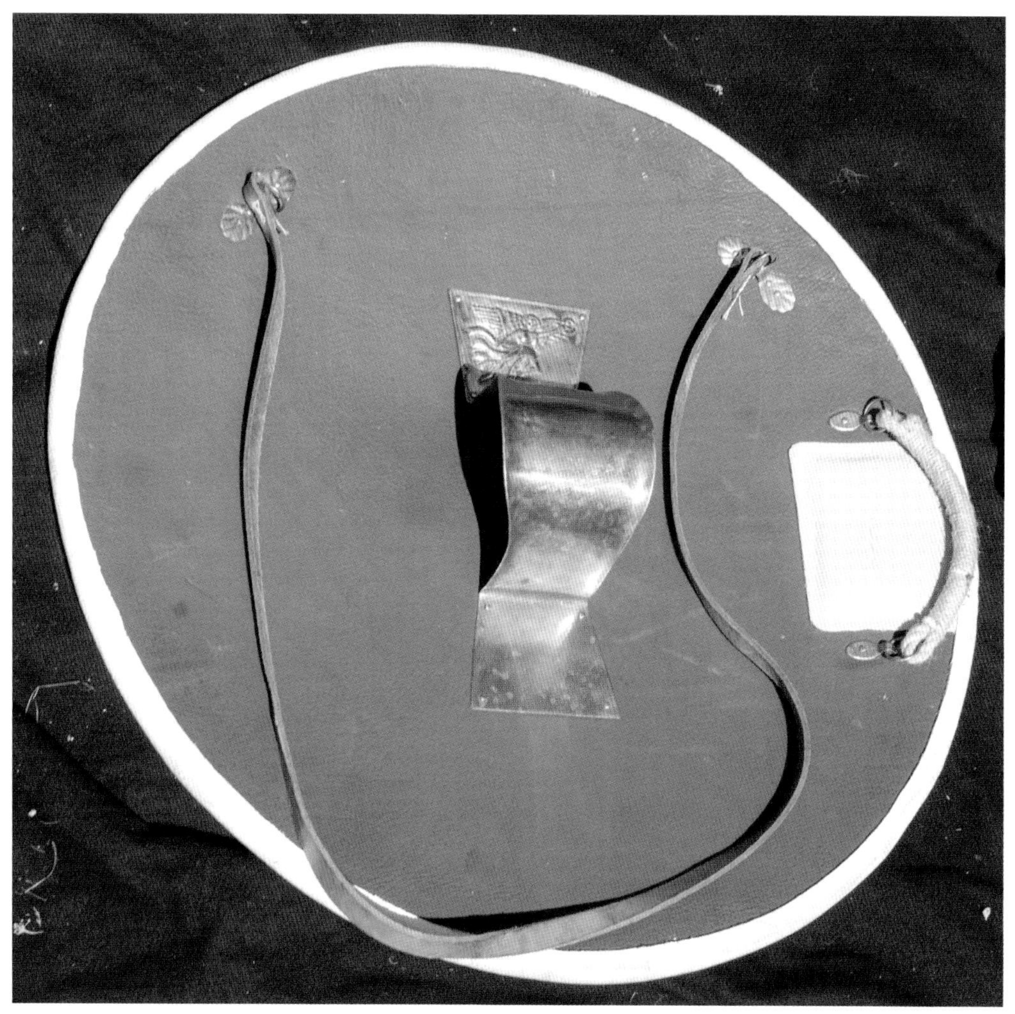

Back of a round pelte shield as used by the foot companions. (*Photo and copyright by Hetairoi*)

fortress, since he considered the Sogdian Rock the safest place for them. The fortress did not have a very large garrison, but it was well provisioned for a long siege. Before attacking, Alexander had asked the defenders to surrender, but these refused and told him that he would need 'men with wings' in order to capture their citadel. The 300 Macedonian volunteers who offered to climb the escarpment in exchange for a reward promised by their king were men with great experience of rock-climbing from previous sieges in the Central Asian campaign, and thus were confident of the outcome of their daunting mission. Using tent-pegs and strong flaxen ropes, the band of soldiers climbed the cliff face at night, losing about thirty men who fell to their deaths during the gruelling ascent. In accordance with their king's orders, they signalled their success to the troops below by waving strips of linen. Alexander then sent a herald to inform the enemy's advanced posts of the hopelessness of their position and to order them to surrender without delay. The defenders, surprised and demoralized by the incredible achievement of the Macedonian climbers, realised they had no option but to submit. Alexander showed humanity towards the captured Sogdians as he was now seeking a durable peace in Central Asia in order to move from Sogdia and start developing further plans of conquest. For these political and strategic reasons he married Roxane, a daughter of Oxyartes, to cement a solid alliance with the tribal rulers of the region. The decisive victory at the Sogdian Rock marked the end of Alexander's Central Asian campaign and of his conquest of the Persian Empire. Nevertheless, the young Macedonian monarch already had in mind another military campaign: his new objective was to conquer all the lands of the known world, starting with India. His soldiers, however, having become extremely

Front of a round hoplon shield. (*Photo and copyright by Hetairoi*)

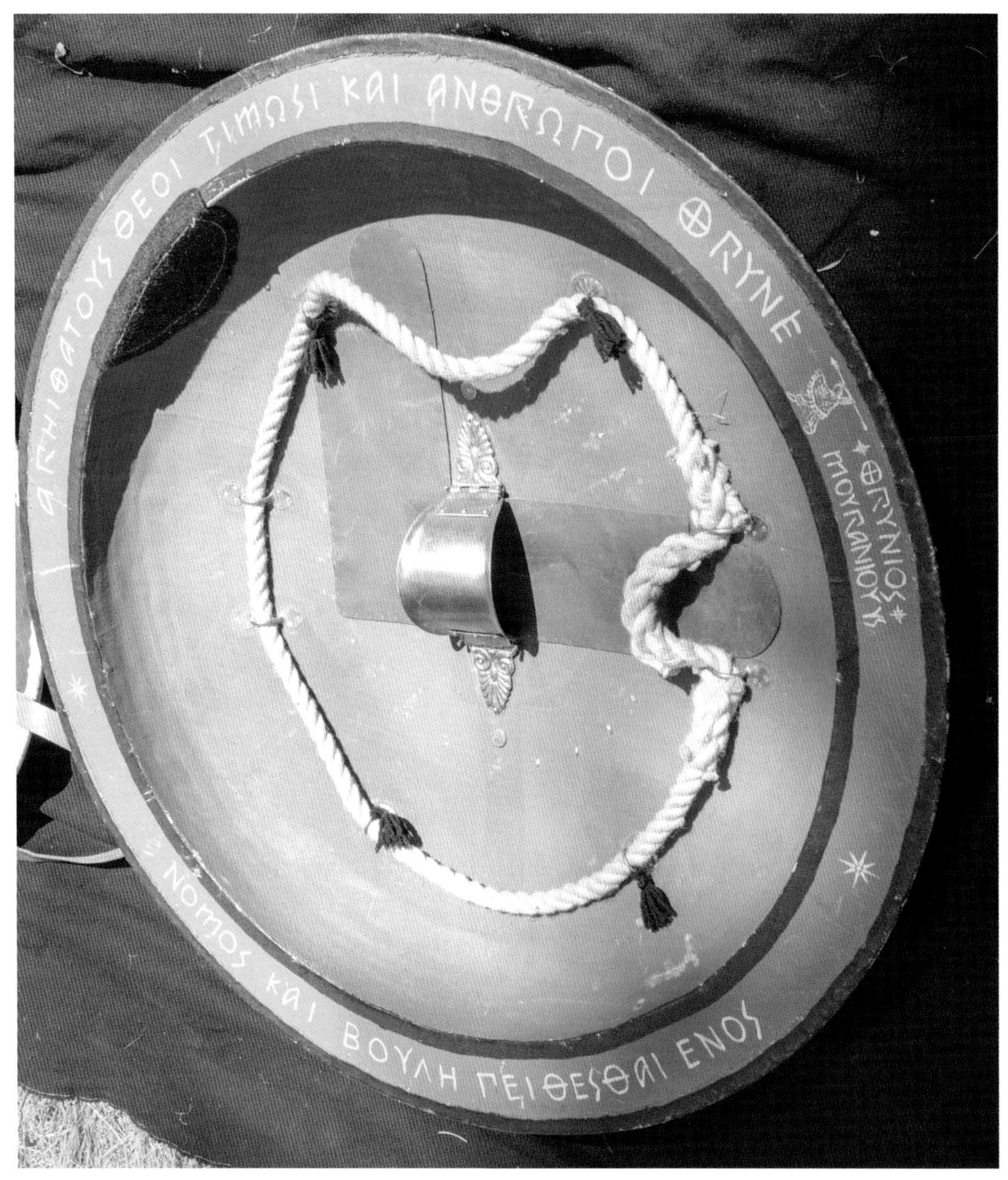

Back of a round hoplon shield. (*Photo and copyright by Hetairoi*)

tired after years of continuous fighting and marching across Asia, believed that their sacrifices should now come to an end: they were ready to go back to their homes in Macedonia and Greece. But Alexander, excited at the idea of conquering a fabulous land such as India, had no intention of stopping and showed little consideration for the requests and feelings of his valorous and loyal veterans. Consequently, the last of his great military campaigns began in 326 BC.

Alexander, now absolute ruler of Asia, presented himself as the direct heir of Darius. He started to claim rights over the territories of northern India (modern Pakistan) that during ancient times had been temporarily submitted by the Persians (forming the so-called Satrapy of Gandhara). These territories had been conquered during the rule of the early Achaemenid monarchs, who reigned after Cyrus the Great, as a result of which some Indian contingents had taken part in the Persian expeditions against Greece. By 400 BC, however, Persian control over the Indian satrapy had gradually receded, and by the time of Alexander's arrival, India was totally independent from any foreign rule. Searching for a pretext to continue his expansion in the Indian sub-continent, Alexander decided to reimpose the rule of the Persian Empire over northern India. He invited all the chieftains of the former Gandhara province to come to him and formally submit to his authority. One of these, the ruler of Taxila named Ambhi, accepted Alexander's request and became an important ally for the Macedonians, since his vast domains between the Indus and the Hydaspes were inhabited by a massive population. The other leaders, however, rejected Alexander's demand and prepared themselves to fight against the invaders from the north. The most important of the Indian rulers who opposed Alexander was Porus, monarch of the powerful Kingdom of Pauravas. Apparently, the kingdoms of Ambhi and Porus were divided by a long regional rivalry, despite having the same ethnic origins, so Alexander's alliance with Taxila soon led to war with the bordering Kingdom of Pauravas. Before descending to the plains of the Punjab to fight against Porus, however, Alexander had to conduct various minor but costly campaigns against the fierce warrior tribes of northern India.

Prior to moving to the immense plains of northern India, it was vital for Alexander to secure his northern flank from possible attacks and raids by the Indian tribes living south of the Pamir and Himalaya mountain ranges. These included three main groups: the Aspasioi of the Kunar Valley, the Guraeans of the Panjkora Valley and the Assakenoi of the Swat and Buner valleys. All these tribes were warlike peoples living on the eastern territories of modern Pakistan. The little-known campaign that Alexander conducted to submit them is called the Cophen campaign from the name of the river that the Macedonians followed during their advance. Alexander instructed the Macedonian forces involved to move rapidly along the Cophen River in order to reach the Indus as soon as possible, while submitting all the cities and villages that they encountered on their route. Once they arrived at the Indus, a formidable natural barrier, the Macedonians would have to build a massive bridge and await the arrival of the bulk of their troops. The first tribe to be attacked by Alexander was that of the Aspasioi, who opposed the Macedonians with all their forces. In the ensuing clash, Alexander was wounded by a dart, but his soldiers were eventually able to defeat the

Crescent-shaped pelte shield of the traditional Thracian type. (*Photo and copyright by Ancient Thrace*)

Aspasioi and raze their capital to the ground. The Guraeans, Alexander's next target, adopted a different strategy, assembling a large army and facing the Macedonians in pitched battle. Despite the great numerical superiority of the Indians, Alexander defeated them at the Battle of Arigaeum, taking over 40,000 prisoners. The attack against the Assakenoi was as rapid and effective as the previous ones, the Macedonians advancing on their capital of Massaga to besiege it. Differently from the other tribes, the Assakenoi had organized a more effective defence, which included bolstering their forces by recruiting 7,000 experienced mercenaries from Indian territories located south of the Indus. With such preparations, the Assakenoi were confident of overcoming the invaders. Indeed, as soon as the Macedonians arrived in front of their capital, their troops launched a surprise attack against them. Considering this sudden assault to be a tactical mistake by the enemy, and seeing the opportunity to defeat them in a pitched battle, Alexander ordered his men to retreat to a hill that was about a mile from the fortified city of Massaga. During their subsequent close pursuit, the Assakenoi lost their discipline and quickly turned into a disordered mass. The Macedonians, who had meanwhile kept perfect order in their ranks, halted their feint retreat on the hill, and when the advancing enemy arrived within range of their missile weapons, Alexander ordered his archers and light troops to attack them. The Assakenoi suffered heavy losses during this phase of the battle, to the point that the

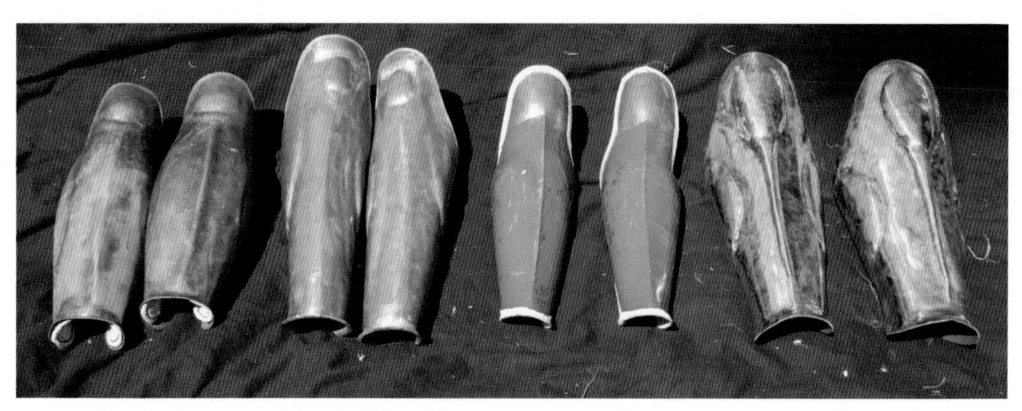

Bronze greaves used by the Macedonian phalangites. (*Photo and copyright by Hetairoi*)

Macedonian light troops passed on to the offensive in order to fully exploit their success. The assault of the light corps was followed by that of the phalanxes, which advanced under the guidance of Alexander (who was once again wounded during this phase of the battle). The remaining Assakenoi warriors and mercenaries were obliged to retreat inside their city, heralding the start of the siege of Massaga. Despite their mastery in siege operations, the Macedonians had great difficulties in taking the well-fortified city. The Indian mercenaries put up a fierce resistance, repulsing various Macedonian attacks and launching raids outside the walls. Alexander's men had to build a siege tower with a long bridge and a terrace in order to attack the enemy walls, but even this was not enough to take the city. Alexander employed the same Macedonian veterans who had stormed Tyre, famous for their heroism and fighting skills, but the defending mercenaries finally surrendered only when their commander was killed by an arrow. The taking of Massaga was not the end of Alexander's campaign against the tribes of northern India: other fortified positions had to be assaulted and conquered, including the stronghold of Aornos. By the summer of 326 BC, however, Alexander had secured his north-eastern flank against any possible menace and his forces were in full control of the Indian valleys south of the Pamir and Himalaya. The Macedonians were now ready to advance into the heart of northern Indian, the Punjab.

The information that we have on the Indian armies of this period is quite scarce, being able to count on only a couple of written sources to reconstruct them: the *Arthasastra* and the *Mahabharata*. The first is a manual on government and warfare attributed to a Maurya minister and dating back to the years that followed Alexander's venture in India, whereas the second is an epic poem dating back to around 200 BC. Despite being written more than a century after Alexander's invasion of India, the *Mahabharata* is full of interesting information for a modern reconstruction of the ancient Indian armies because it describes Indian warfare of a previous era exactly as

Different models of bronze greaves. (*Photo and copyright by Athenea Prómakhos*)

the *Iliad* (written around 800 BC) recounts Mycenaean warfare of 1,200 BC. At the time of Porus, Indian armies included four different categories of troops: infantry, cavalry, chariots and elephants. The infantry element was the most numerous, while chariots and elephants were the most prestigious. The *Mahabharata* gives proportions of one elephant to one chariot, three cavalrymen and five infantrymen. According to Arrian, our main and most reliable source for the campaigns of Alexander in India, the army raised by Porus and deployed at the Battle of the Hydaspes included 200 elephants, 420 chariots (each with a crew of six men), 6,000 cavalry and 30,000 infantry. While an impressive army for the standards of the time, it was not particularly so for Indian ones: at more or less the same time, the Nanda Empire, the greatest state of the age in India, could field an immense army with 3,000 elephants, 2,000 chariots, 20,000 cavalry and 200,000 footmen. From a tactical point of view, the infantry and cavalry had no active or significant roles on the battlefield: their main function was to protect the elephants and chariots by performing auxiliary duties. Each elephant or chariot received a certain number of infantry and cavalry. Indian armies usually also included contingents of mercenaries, fighting as archers or light infantrymen. The main difference between the tribal armies of northern India and those of the bigger states located in the plains was in the number of elephants and chariots: due to the geographical nature of their territory, the northern tribes living in modern Pakistan had no chariots and very few elephants. With the notable exception of the nobles going to the battlefield on elephants or chariots, all the Indian warriors wore no kind of personal protection. All components of the army were lightly equipped:

Good example of bronze greaves. (*Photo and copyright by Athenea Prómakhos*)

the cavalry was entirely made up of mounted javelineers, while the infantry included front-rank soldiers, javelineers and archers. The front-rank soldiers were armed with spears and tall body-shields, but had no helmets or cuirasses; the foot javelineers, like the mounted ones, were equipped with smaller shields and with javelins, and made up the largest part of the infantry. The archers were the real elite force of the Indian infantry, their tactical superiority being down to the excellence of their main weapon: a heavy and powerful bamboo bow, 1.5 metres tall and having a hemp or sinew string that was drawn to the ear. Arrows were three cubits long, made of cane or reed and flighted with vulture feathers. Their heads were usually made of iron or horn. Sometimes these could be poisoned: apparently the use of poison arrows was forbidden in the wars that were fought between Indian states, but it seems they were employed against Alexander's invaders. Kings and nobles, fighting on elephants or chariots, were armed with javelins or spears and were protected by brass helmets and scale armour of very simple manufacture. As secondary weapons, the Indian warriors of Alexander's times had swords and maces or clubs. The former had a broad blade that was three cubits long and were used for powerful two-handed cutting blows, brought down from above the head. Maces and clubs could be used in one hand, two hands or thrown; according to ancient sources, the Indian fighters were very good at using these primitive but effective weapons. The Macedonians thus faced a large force of lightly equipped infantry that comprised elite contingents of charioteers and archers plus the devastating 'shock' force of the elephant corps.

The bulk of the Macedonian Army entered northern India from the Khyber Pass, while a smaller force under command of Alexander marched south from a more northerly route. After combining with the allied army of Taxila, the Macedonian forces advanced against Porus and his kingdom. According to the historian Arrian, Porus was at the head of one of the most significant regional powers of northern India. He describes Porus as a remarkable man, especially for his personal strength (apparently he was very tall) and his courage. Undoubtedly, Porus was a military leader of great experience, and as soon as Alexander formed an alliance with Taxila, he started mobilizing an impressive army to face the Macedonians on the battlefield. Unlike the northern tribes that had just been conquered by Alexander, Porus could not use mountains or a complex of fortified cities to slow down the advance of the invaders: his kingdom was located on the plains of Punjab, so his only strategic choice was to defeat the enemy with an army of superior numbers. Porus deployed his forces along the Hydaspes River (the modern Jhelum River), which marked the border between his realm and that of Taxila. The Indian king believed that Alexander would wait for the monsoon season to end before attempting to cross the river with all his forces, so he was confident of being able to gain more time to recruit additional troops. During the monsoon, being swollen by the melting snows of the Himalaya, the Hydaspes was over a mile wide. It was also quite deep and extremely fast moving: an incredible natural barrier, which could be defended with a limited number of men. Porus' plans would have proved to be perfect in an Indian war, but he was facing a different kind of opponent who did not use reason according to local standards. Alexander made camp on the opposite bank of the river, exactly in front of Porus' defensive positions on the eastern side of the Hydaspes. He gave his enemies every indication that he would wait for the monsoon season to end, for example by having large shipments of food and supplies sent in from his allies of Taxila. In reality, Alexander had no intention of waiting. His army was smaller than that of his Indian opponent, but included some of the best Macedonian troops. In addition, Alexander had recruited some new contingents of troops from the warrior peoples that he had submitted across Asia. The army deployed by Alexander at the Hydaspes was without doubt the least 'Macedonian' one ever guided by the young king. His military forces were gradually transforming themselves into a multi-national contingent, but the core of which remained the Macedonian phalanxes and heavy cavalry. The new Asiatic troops raised by Alexander were going to play a fundamental role in the forthcoming battle. He understood that some military traditions of the conquered peoples could

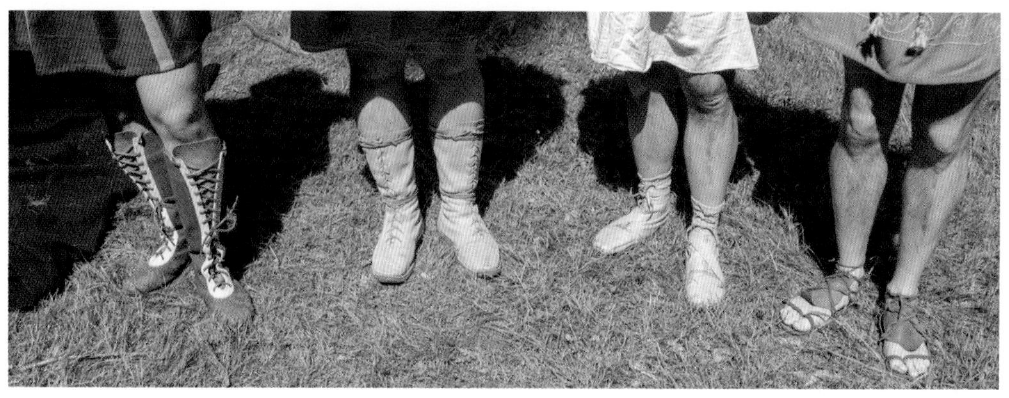

Different models of Macedonian cavalry boots and infantry sandals. (*Photo and copyright by Hetairoi*)

be used for the benefit of his army, and thus had started to gradually transform the Macedonian military machine.

Generally speaking, the new infantry recruited from the Asiatic provinces were trained and equipped in the usual fashion of the Macedonian phalangites (they were the *epigoni*), which caused some anger among the Macedonian veterans but enabled Alexander to enlarge his infantry corps. The Asiatic cavalry, instead, was recruited to fight in its traditional fashion, so Alexander did not try to transform it into a heavy force like the Macedonian horsemen. He understood that the real excellence of the eastern cavalry consisted of the light mounted javelineers and archers: for this reason he tried to recruit as many mounted auxiliary units as possible, anticipating their vital use against the war elephants of the Indian armies. Alexander knew full well that Porus had some strategic and tactical advantages: differently from him, the Indian king could wait for months on the banks of the river, because his supply line was extremely short. In addition, it was enough for Porus to guard the best potential crossing spots and destroy the Macedonian forces as they emerged from the river. To give false impressions to his opponents, Alexander built numerous campfires along his side of the river, marching his men back and forth in formation. Meanwhile, his explorers were already searching for the most suitable crossing spot. Initially, Porus' forces followed each movement of the enemy on the opposite bank, but the Indian

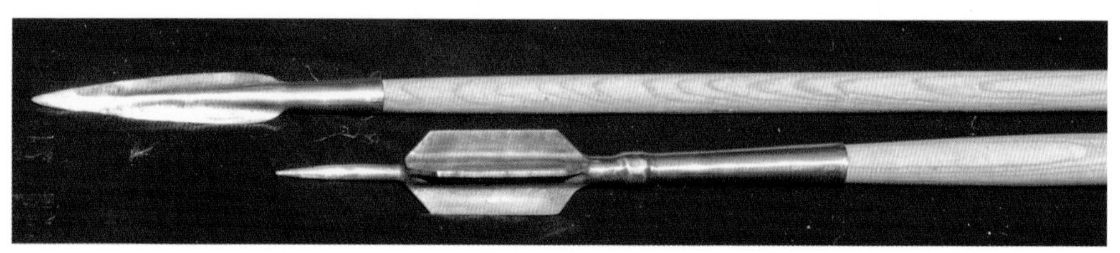

Detail of a sarissa pike's point and spike. (*Photo and copyright by Hetairoi*)

king soon believed that these were only diversions aimed at distracting his forces. After a long and tedious search, a suitable location to cross was found about 18 miles from the Macedonian camp, at a bend of the river in a heavily wooded area that would be perfect to provide cover for the advancing troops. It was a late evening in May 326 BC and a terrible thunderstorm was raging. Despite the bad weather, however, Alexander's army was ready to cross the Hydaspes. To keep Porus unaware of his moves, Alexander left his general Craterus in the Macedonian camp with a large reserve force, with orders to cross the river only at a later stage of the forthcoming battle. The crossing of Alexander's main attacking force was divided into three waves. In order to safely cross the river, the Macedonians made rafts from their tents and used thirty boats. In total, an estimated 15,000 cavalry and 11,000 infantry crossed the Hydaspes. Unfortunately, the crossing did not go exactly as planned, as instead of reaching the opposite shore, the Macedonian soldiers landed on a large island in the middle of the river. The troops had to swim from the island to the far bank, since there was not enough space to use the boats. After reaching the opposite shore at dawn, Alexander regrouped his forces and put them in battle order. Some of the infantry had not yet completed the crossing, but Alexander advanced nonetheless. A defensive screen of Asiatic mounted archers (notably Scythian ones) was placed in front of the advancing army, in order to protect the rest of the troops from the attacks of Porus' elephants. After the light cavalry came the Macedonian horse companions, which were Alexander's main attacking force since the phalanxes and the other infantry units were only partially deployed in battle order and several of their corps were still crossing the river. The scouts of Porus saw the movements of the Macedonians over the Hydaspes, and immediately informed their king of Alexander's arrival.

Taken by surprise, Porus tried to gain some time in order to deploy his troops in order of battle. For this purpose he sent a contingent of 3,000 mounted men and 120 chariots against the Macedonians, under guidance of his son. This chosen force fought with great courage, but was easily destroyed by Alexander's veteran heavy cavalry, with the son of Porus being killed in the clash. Alexander advanced for 6 miles towards the Indian camp and then stopped, waiting for the remainder of his infantry to arrive. According to Arrian, Alexander had no intention of making the fresh enemy troops a present of his own breathless and exhausted men, so he paused before launching the final attack. Meanwhile, Porus had time to start the deployment of his troops, with the elephants placed in the front line, ahead of the massed infantry, and the cavalry on the right and left flanks together with the six-man war chariots. Porus positioned himself in the middle of the Indian line, mounted on his elephant. The deployment of Alexander's troops was identical to that of Porus: the phalanxes were in the middle, with a screen of mounted archers and light cavalrymen in front of

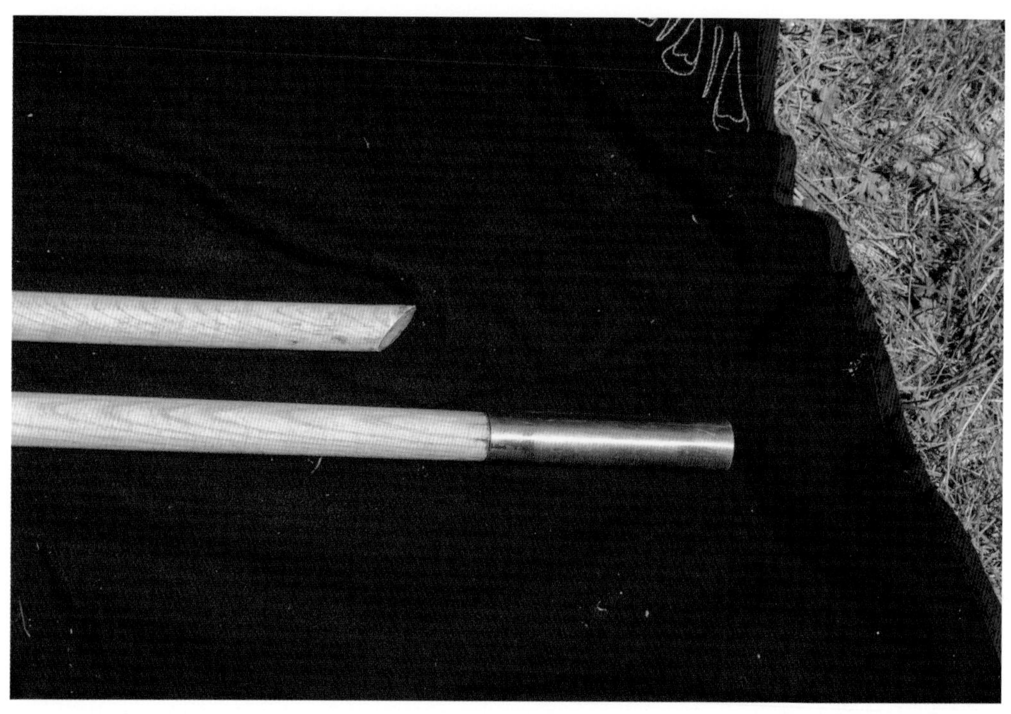

Central part of a sarissa pike, where the two parts of the weapon were joined together. (*Photo and copyright by Hetairoi*)

Points of Macedonian spears. (*Photo and copyright by Athenea Prómakhos*)

them; on the right and left wings, he deployed his cavalry. The right wing was under his own command and the left was led by Coenus.

With both sides now deployed, the battle commenced. While his light cavalry screen pelted the Indian elephants with a furious rain of javelins and arrows, Alexander's flanks attacked the two enemy wings. Coenus' assault against Porus' right caused no particular difficulties for the Indians, who were able to contain the Macedonian cavalry, but on Porus' left wing the cavalry charge led by Alexander destroyed the Indian mounted troops. To deal with the emergency on his left wing, Porus sent part of his cavalry from the right to circle back and help their comrades against Alexander. Soon after this, he ordered a general advance of his elephants against the Macedonian phalanxes. For the first time in the military history of the ancient world, a western fighting force faced the power of war elephants. In Indian warfare, elephants were employed in battle mostly against cavalry, because horses had a terrible fear of the pachyderms and could not stand their strong smell. This time, however, the elephants were facing a compact mass of heavy infantry. The psychological impact of the charge was unpredictable: it was a first for the Macedonians as well as for the elephants. The initial assault of the war beasts was devastating, with the Macedonians suffering heavy losses and the phalanxes, surprised by the size of the 'monsters' that they were facing, seeming to be on the point of breaking. After the initial panic, however, Alexander's veteran infantry started to reorganize themselves. They gradually began to pull back, but without breaking their ranks. Meanwhile, Alexander's Asiatic light cavalry continued to attack the elephants on their vulnerable flanks, together with some task forces of light infantry who attacked their legs. The wounds caused by the enemy javelins and arrows (especially to the eyes) began to take effect on the Indian elephants, which were blocked to the front by the phalanx and harassed on the flanks by the Macedonian light troops. The pachyderms of Porus became tired, their charges grew feebler and they soon started to panic, causing more damage to the Indian infantry placed behind them than to the opposing phalanxes. The retreat of the elephants caused serious losses to the Indian infantry, opening large holes in Porus' front line. The phalangites then advanced against the lightly equipped Indian infantry, who soon fell into complete disarray. At the same time, Coenus, having been able to defeat the cavalry of Porus on the right wing, moved around the rear of the Indian forces. The left flank of Porus, which was already facing the charge of Alexander, was now attacked from the rear by Coenus' cavalry and completely destroyed. Blocked from behind, Porus' army could flee from the ensuing massacre only by crossing the Hydaspes, but Craterus had by now advanced with his own troops and had crossed the river, enclosing the Indians in the perfect trap that had been prepared by Alexander. At the end of the battle, seeing the complete destruction of his army, Porus remained on the field on his elephant: despite suffering severe wounds, he could not accept defeat. Alexander, full of admiration for Porus, approached the proud and defeated king with the intention of saving his life. He asked Porus how he wanted to be treated, and the Indian leader responded that he wanted to be treated as a king. Alexander respected this request and told Porus that he would remain king of his realm but as an ally of the Macedonians. Porus accepted and thus became satrap of his own kingdom, which was enlarged with the inclusion of the territories conquered by Alexander during the Cophen campaign.

The Battle of the Hydaspes had been an extremely violent affair, the most terrible clash in Alexander's military career and probably his most difficult victory. Losses had been terrible for the Indians, who suffered more than 20,000 men killed, while the Macedonians also suffered terrible casualties by their usual standards. They had lost more than 1,000 men, which while appearing to be a small figure for so large an army as the Macedonians fielded, it should be borne in mind that in their previous battles against the Persians, the army of Alexander had always lost only a very limited number of men. Among the Macedonian casualties was Bucephalus, the beloved horse of Alexander. Consequently, on the site of the battle, Alexander built the city of Alexandria Bucephalous in honour and memory of the horse which he had tamed and which had followed him since his first adventures.

The Battle of the Hydaspes was the final battle in Alexander's incredible military career. His soldiers, by now too tired to continue the conquest of India, had no

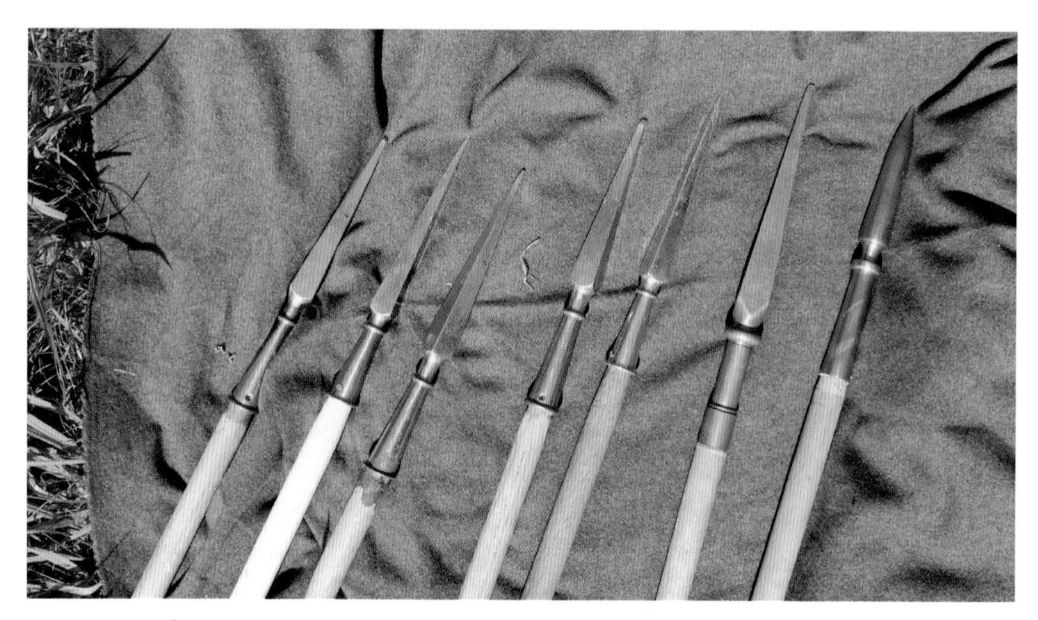

Spikes of Macedonian spears. (*Photo and copyright by Athenea Prómakhos*)

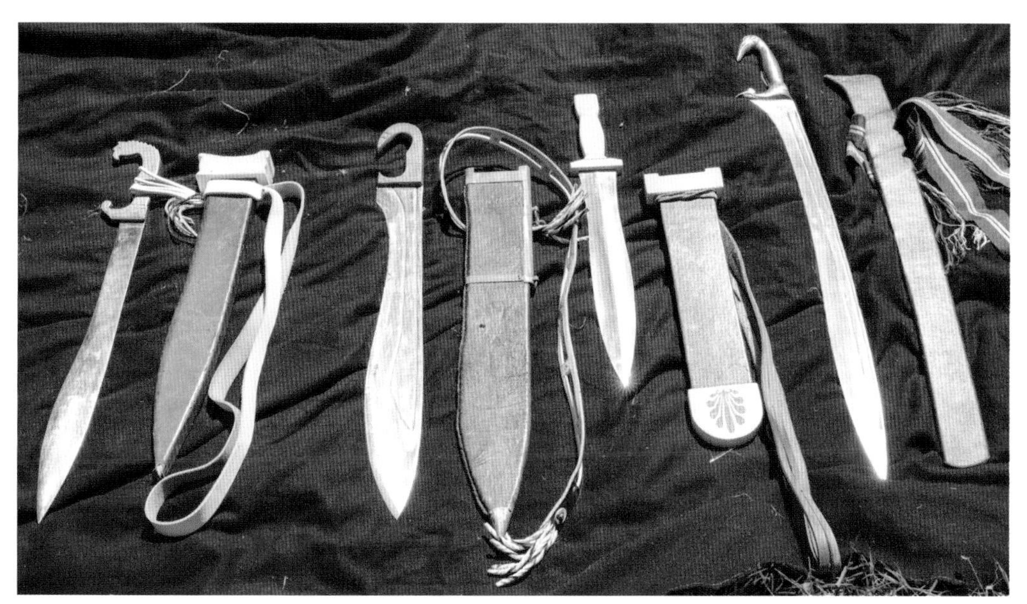

Two kopis swords (left), along with a xiphos sword (centre) and another kopis sword (right). (*Photo and copyright by Hetairoi*)

intention of facing other Indian armies that could comprise even larger contingents of war elephants. To continue the advance in India they would have had to cross the Ganges River, much larger and deeper than the Hydaspes, and face the army of the Nanda Empire (which was expecting them with 3,000 elephants, 2,000 chariots, 20,000 cavalry and 200,000 infantry). For the first time in his life, Alexander was defeated: the Macedonian soldiers were finally able to bend the strong will of their king, obliging him to return to Babylon. They had reached the edge of the known world and crossed several regions that no other Greek before them had ever visited. Most of the Macedonian Army left India by marching north across south-eastern Iran in order to reach Babylon and Mesopotamia. Alexander, however, built a large fleet on the coastline of India and embarked some of his troops on it. The Macedonian ships, commanded by Nearchus, were ordered to explore the Persian Gulf and the eastern coastline of Arabia before moving to present-day Kuwait and landing the soldiers transported on them. The long march across northern India was particularly difficult for Alexander and the bulk of his land forces, since the Macedonians took a new route that crossed the vast Gedrosian Desert. The loyal veterans who had left Macedonia and Greece many years before were determined to see their families and their homes again after a life of war, but hundreds of them died in the harsh desert areas of India. Once in Babylon, Alexander paid off the debts of all his soldiers as a gesture of thanks and sent back to their homes most of his older veterans. During this period he adopted Persian customs and started to wear the traditional clothes

Xiphos sword (left) and four kopis swords (right). (*Photo and copyright by Hetairoi*)

of the Achaemenid monarchs. Meanwhile, he planned to increase the number of *epigoni* in his army and introduced many Persian nobles to his royal court. Alexander wanted to create a new multi-cultural civilization by melding the traditions of the Macedonians and Greeks with those of the Persians, but such acts were perceived as offensive by many of his subordinates and caused the outbreak of several revolts. Alexander was able to restore order to his army and find a compromise with his men, but his dreams of cultural integration were still far from being realized. He organized a mass marriage between some of his best Macedonian commanders and Persian noblewomen, but this did not have the positive results he had hoped for, with no effective fusion between the two cultures. Then, during the night of 10 June 323 BC,

Alexander died in Babylon, probably of malaria or typhoid fever, aged just 32. In just a few years he had conquered the largest empire in the history of Antiquity and had won more battles than any other Hellenic general. A man was dead, but a legend was then born.

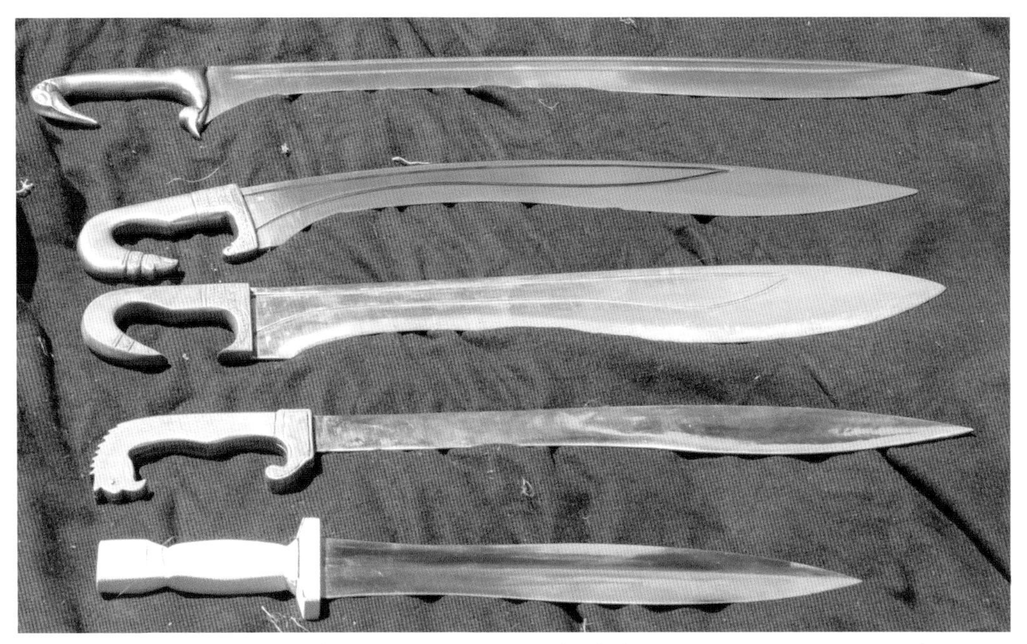

Xiphos sword (bottom) and four kopis swords (top). (*Photo and copyright by Hetairoi*)

Chapter 6

Weapons and Equipment of the Macedonian Army

The main offensive weapon of the Macedonian phalangites was the sarissa pike, an 'over-long' spear about 4–6 metres in length. The sarissa, introduced by Iphicrates for his "reformed" hoplites, was perfected by Philip II and completely replaced the traditional hoplite spear (the dory) inside the Macedonian infantry. In general terms, the sarissa was superior to the dory in one important aspect: being much longer than the latter, which was only some 2–3 metres in length, it extended the rows of overlapping spears projecting from the infantry formations towards the enemy and thus made the infantry phalanxes much stronger than before. The sarissa was made of tough and resilient cornel wood, which was particularly hard but also very heavy; each pike weighed approximately 5.5–6.5kg. It had a sharp iron head shaped like a leaf and a bronze butt-spike that could be fixed to the ground when defensive formations were deployed. The spike was also sharpened so that it could be used to pierce an enemy shield just like the head of the sarissa. The spike, which was made of bronze in order to protect it from rust, had a very important function as it balanced the whole sarissa and made it easier to wield for the infantrymen. It could also be used as a 'back-up' point in case the main one broke during combat. The sheer bulk and length of the sarissa required the phalangites to use it with both hands, allowing them to carry only a 60cm round pelte shield suspended from the neck to cover their left shoulder. The pelte shield was very small and light, being of some use only against enemy arrows. Indeed, the main defence for the phalangites was the offensive potential of their pikes. Engaging a Macedonian infantryman in close combat was not easy for a Greek hoplite or a Persian foot soldier, since he first had to get past the wall of enemy pikes before coming into contact with the phalangites. Outside the tight formation of the phalanx, however, the sarissa was of no use: it was very heavy and slowed down the movement of its user. It was composed of two lengths and was carried dismantled, on the shoulders, during marches. The pike was joined by a central bronze tube only when needed, shortly before the beginning of a battle. Intensive training allowed the phalangites to wield their pikes in unison, swinging them vertically to wheel about and then lowering them to the horizontal. The uniform 'swish' produced by this movement of the Macedonian pikes daunted many enemies and thus was a kind of psychological weapon. The foot companions were deployed in their usual close formation only when they reached the battlefield. Their wall of pikes had five rows of sarissae projecting in front of the first line. The back rows of each phalanx, which could not hit the enemy, bore their pikes angled upwards in readiness, and could rapidly fill any gaps opened by enemy arrows inside the phalanx. The practice of bearing the sarissae of the back rows angled upwards had the additional purpose of deflecting incoming arrows.

The horse companions of the Macedonian heavy cavalry used a peculiar kind of cavalry spear, which was known as the xyston. This was a long thrusting weapon that measured about 3.5–4.5 metres, with a solid wooden shaft and a point at both ends. The butt-spike, like that of the sarissa, was to counter-balance the weight of the head and could be used as a 'back-up' when the latter was broken during combat. The xyston heavy cavalry spear could be wielded either underarm or overarm. In addition, considering its large dimensions, it could be employed with both hands by its user, especially just prior to hitting a target. Judging from its general features and tactical use, the Macedonian xyston was probably a Hellenic copy of the Scythian kontus spear, which was used with great success by the heavy cavalry of several steppe tribes. The light troops of the Macedonian Army, be they on foot or mounted, were all armed with throwing javelins. These had a very simple point made of metal (having the shape of a leaf) and were 1–1.5 metres long. They were extremely light and had no butt-spike. Neither the Macedonian heavy cavalry nor light cavalry used shields, while the light infantrymen had the pelte shield of the traditional kind designed by the Thracians. This was made of wicker or wood and was covered with goatskin or sheepskin. It was usually carried with an arm strap and with a handle at the rim, but could also be transported on the back, being slung through the use of a back strap. On the back of the shield there was a simple central grip. The pelte was the key to the tactical success of Macedonian light infantrymen: it was designed for a fighter who had to throw javelins and was perfectly suited to protect its user from enemy missile weapons.

The hypaspists carried the same dory spear and hoplon shield as the traditional Greek hoplites. The dory was 2–3 metres long and both its head and butt were made of iron. The blade of the head was leaf-shaped, while the spike at the butt's end was very thin and could be used to strike as well as to fix the spear into the terrain. The round hoplon shield was also known as the Argive shield, and its introduction during the last decades of the Greek Dark Ages marked the beginning of the so-called hoplite revolution. This kind of shield was markedly convex and had a reinforced rim. In addition, it had an innovative grip that made its use particularly effective, consisting of an arm band fitted to the centre of the shield on the back. The hoplite put his left forearm through the band and the shield was thus easily fastened. This

Nice example of xiphos short sword. (*Photo and copyright by Athenea Prómakhos*)

simple but innovative system was completed by the presence of a strap (which worked as a handgrip) near the rim: this was grasped with the left hand by the hoplite, which made it difficult for an enemy to loosen the hypaspist's grip on the shield during close combat. These basic characteristics of the Argive shield, together with its dimensions (80–100cm in diameter, covering each soldier from the chin to the knee), were a major

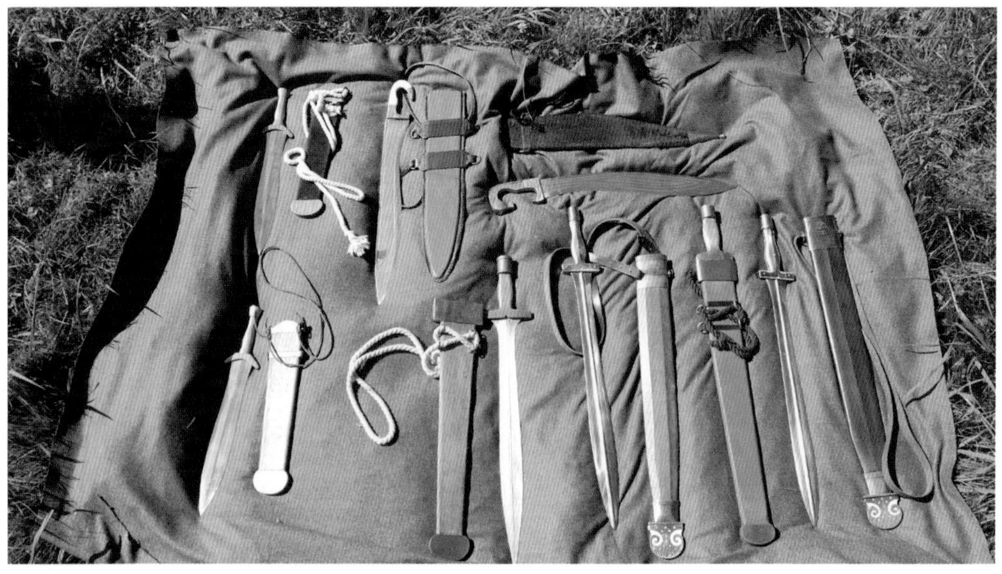

Two xiphos swords (top and bottom left), two kopis swords (top right) and four machaira swords (bottom right). (*Photo and copyright by Athenea Prómakhos*)

factor in the tactics employed by the hoplites. Half of the hoplon always protruded beyond the left-hand side of its user and thus could protect the right-hand side of the man fighting next to him. If the hoplites were well trained and if a soldier had a good degree of coordination with the two comrades fighting by his side, the hoplite phalanx worked perfectly as an impenetrable wall of shields. Each shield was made of hardwood and was covered with bronze or ox-hide on the external surface. The rim and the arm band were made of bronze, whereasd all the other fittings attached to the back of it, including the hand grip, were made of rawhide or felt. The back of the shield was lined with leather. The standard weight of a hoplon was in the region of 7kg. The external surface could be painted with an infinite variety of symbols and decorations. The hoplon remained the same for many years and did not change any of its main features. The only innovation introduced after the Persian Wars was the use of a leather curtain that was attached to the bottom part of the shield in order to protect the hoplite's legs from enemy arrows. During the campaigns against the Persian invaders, many Greek infantrymen were wounded in that part of the body that was not protected by either the shield or the armour. Leather curtains became quite popular and were employed extensively by mercenary hoplites operating in Asia. Later, when the practice of wearing greaves around the shins fell into disuse, the curtains started to be commonly used in Greece.

A fundamental element in the defensive equipment of a Macedonian foot companion or horse companion was his body armour. By the time of Philip II's conquest of Greece, one of the most popular kinds of armour was the muscle cuirass, which was made of bronze and had its external surface sculpted with great detail in order to reproduce the anatomy of the torso. This model of corselet could be quite short, reaching the waist, or could be long enough to cover the whole abdomen. It consisted of two separate plates made of bronze, which were joined together with hinges at the sides and at the shoulders (one half of the hinge was attached to the front plate and the other half to the back plate). Usually there were six hinges on each cuirass: two on each side and one for each shoulder. On either side of each hinge there was a ring that was used to pull the two plates of the cuirass together. The muscle cuirass became increasingly unpopular over time, to the point that by the end of Alexander's reign, linen had become the standard material for producing corselets. By the time of the Persian Wars, the Greeks had already started to use linen or leather to manufacture pteruges: these were strips or lappets that were assembled together to form a sort of defensive skirt which could be worn under the bronze cuirass. Since they proved to be extremely effective, especially against enemy arrows, the pteruges soon became popular and also began to be employed to protect the shoulders and upper arms (being worn under the muscle cuirass on the shoulders).

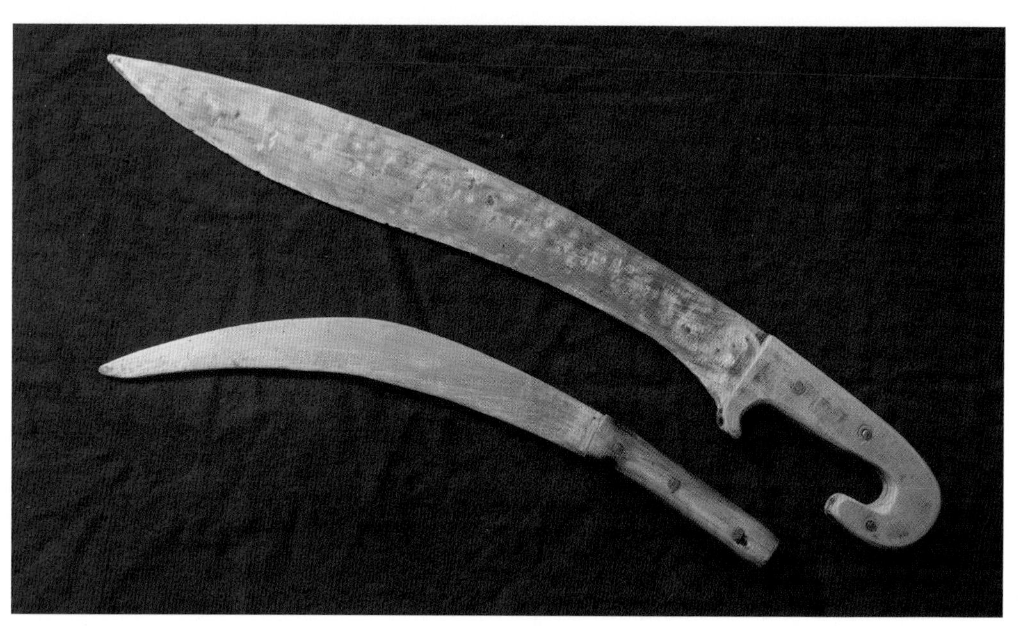

Curved knife and kopis sword of the kind used by Thracian warriors. (*Photo and copyright by Ancient Thrace*)

The linen cuirass – a corselet entirely made of linen – was already in use during the Persian Wars and had the great advantage of being particularly light and easy to wear. It consisted of multiple layers of linen pressed and glued together in order to form a corselet about 0.5cm thick. This extended down to the hips, and its lower part, going below the waist, had slits in order to make it easy to bend forward. These slits formed a line of pteruges, which were part of the main cuirass and not a separate component of it. Under the main corselet, another layer was worn: this also had pteruges but was stuck on the inside of the cuirass in such a way that it covered the gaps in the pteruges of the outer layer. The whole corselet was produced as a single-piece and thus was wrapped around the torso before being tied together on the left side. A specifically designed U-shaped plate (also made of linen) was worn on the shoulders; this was fixed to the back of the corselet and pulled forward to protect the front part of the shoulders. Soon after the appearance of the linen cuirass, the Greeks created an updated version which was known as a composite cuirass. Basically, this was a standard linen cuirass that was reinforced by adding bronze scales on its external

Light infantry throwing javelins. (*Photo and copyright by Hetairoi*)

surface. These scales were usually assembled into a large band placed around the waist, but they could also be placed on other points of the corselet (such as the shoulders or the loins). Sometimes a linen corselet could be entirely covered with bronze scales, but these costly examples of composite cuirass were quite rare. The body protection of a phalangite was usually completed by a pair of bronze greaves, which also covered the knees and were worn together with sandals. They could be decorated in many different ways, for example reproducing the anatomy of the lower leg or with geometric patterns, and could be pulled open and clipped on to the leg or strapped on the back.

The defensive equipment of the Macedonian heavy infantry and heavy cavalry was completed by the helmet, which was made of bronze and could have several different shapes. In all, seven different models of helmet were used by the Macedonian soldiers under Philip II and Alexander: the Corinthian, Chalcidian, Attic, Phrygian/Thracian, Boeotian, Pilos and Konos helmets. The Corinthian helmet was introduced during the last phase of the Greek Dark Ages and remained the most popular model for much of the early Classical period. As is clear from its name, it was probably initially designed in Corinth. It included a frontal plate that covered the entire face, providing excellent protection for the wearer. This frontal plate had three thin slits: two for the eyes and a vertical one for the mouth and nose. On the back, a large curved projection of the helmet protected the nape of the neck. When not fighting, a soldier would wear his Corinthian helmet tipped upward for comfort, thereby freeing most of his face from the frontal plate (which would have assumed an oblique position). One of the main characteristics of the Corinthian helmet was the presence of an indentation in the bottom edge dividing the jawline from the neckline. Over time, however, this was replaced by a simple dart. The greatest fault of the Corinthian helmets was that they made hearing practically impossible, so the surface of the helmet over the ears started to be cut away. Before adopting this solution, several experiments were made, which led to the creation of a new helmet that derived directly from the Corinthian one: the Chalcidian helmet. This was lighter and less bulky than the Corinthian helmet, since it left the entire face and ears of the wearer completely free (there was no frontal plate). Consequently, hearing and vision were much better compared to its precursor. The Chalcidian helmet consisted of a hemispherical dome, under which there were a pair of cheek pieces and a neck guard, while on the front there was a very small nasal bar. The cheek pieces could be fixed or hinged to the helmet. Adornments and protuberances of various kinds could be attached to the top of the helmet's dome. Various experiments were also made to improve the Chalcidian helmet, and these led to the introduction of a new design known as the Attic helmet. This was one of the last models of helmet to be developed during the Classical period and also

Points of three javelins and one spear. (*Photo and copyright by Ancient Thrace*)

Macedonian sling. (*Photo and copyright by Ancient Thrace*)

had widespread diffusion during the subsequent Hellenistic period. In general terms, the Attic helmet was similar to the Chalcidian one, but did not have the latter's nose guard. Its cheek pieces were hinged and not fixed, as in the later examples of Chalcidian helmet. The Attic helmet soon became extremely popular and started to be decorated in a variety of different ways: these included incisions, adornments and protuberances of various kinds that were sculpted or applied on its external surface.

The Phrygian/Thracian, Boeotian and Pilos helmets all derived from soft caps that were worn by the Macedonians and Greeks during their daily life. The first model, the Phrygian/Thracian helmet, started to be produced after the Greeks came into close contact with the warriors inhabiting Thrace and Phrygia, a region of Anatolia populated by a warlike community of Thracian stock that had migrated to Asia Minor during the Archaic period of Greek history. As a result, both the Thracians and Phrygians wore the same distinct soft cap, which had a high and forward-inclined apex. The model of helmet deriving from this cap had this same apex and was characterized by the presence of a peak at the front, which shaded the wearer's eyes and offered some additional protection. Sometimes, instead of the peak, a Phrigyan/Thracian helmet could have a small nasal bar similar to the one on the Chalcidian helmets. A couple of large cheek pieces were attached to the main body of the helmet; frequently these were large enough to form a facial mask with only three small gaps for the eyes and nose/mouth. When the cheek pieces were large and tied together to form this mask, the overall appearance of the helmet was not so different from that of the Corinthian one. The Boeotian helmet, as indicated by its name, was first developed in the region of Boeotia. Despite being largely used by Theban hoplites, it eventually became extremely common as a cavalry helmet. From many points of view, it was perfect for cavalry use: it was completely open on the face, allowed good peripheral vision and permitted unimpaired hearing. The Boeotian helmet consisted of a domed skull surrounded by a wide and flaring down-sloping brim. The brim came down at the rear to protect the back of the neck but also projected forward over the forehead to work as a sort of visor. On the sides, the brim had a complex shape, comprising downward-pointing folds that offered some protection to the lateral areas of the face. The Boeotian helmet was in essence a bronze version of the regular petasos sun hat, which was widely employed by the famous Thessalian cavalry. This kind of helmet was usually decorated with a falling horsehair plume instead of a crest. The Pilos helmet was a bronze version of the cap of the same name, which was worn by most of the Greek and Macedonian peasants during their everyday life. The pilos was a brimless skullcap made of felt, having a simple conical shape. When at war, Hellenic soldiers generally wore their pilos under the helmet for more comfort. As a result, a new model of helmet with exactly the same shape as the cap started to be developed. This was very comfortable to wear and easy to produce, to the point that by the end of the Peloponnesian War it had become the most common model of helmet produced in Greece. The Pilos helmet was quite tall and thus offered good protection for an infantryman against cavalry. Additionally, it was completely open and gave full vision to its wearer (it only had a small visor around the opening). The Konos helmet was the last model of helmet developed during the Classical period and was in large use during the Hellenistic period. Basically, it was a variation of the Pilos helmet, with two main peculiarities: instead of the visor, it had a thin brim protruding from the base and closely fitting around the wearer's head, and also had bronze ear guards that hung to the jawbone. In practice, it was a Pilos helmet with the characteristic brim of a Boeotian one.

The Macedonian foot companions and horse companions used two different models of sword, both short and made of iron: the kopis and the xiphos. The kopis was a heavy cutting sword with a forward-curving blade, the latter being single-edged. One-handed, the kopis had a blade length of 48–65cm, which pitched forward towards the point and was concave on the part located nearest to the hilt. The peculiar recurved shape of the kopis made it capable of delivering a blow with the same power as an axe. A peculiar version of the kopis, known as the machaira, also existed: this had all the same features, but its blade was not recurved. The kopis was particularly popular as a cavalry weapon due to the peculiar shape of its blade, while the Machaira was primarily an infantry sword. The universal sword of the phalangites, however, was the xiphos, a one-handed and double-edged short sword with straight blade measuring between 45 and 60cm. It usually had a midrib and was diamond or lenticular in cross-section. The xiphos had a long point and thus was an excellent thrusting weapon specifically designed for close combat.

Bibliography

Primary sources
Arrian, *Anabasis of Alexander*
Arrian, *Indike*
Arrian, *Tactics*
Asklepiodotos, *Tactics*
Diodorus Siculus, *History*
Pausanias, *Guide to Greece*
Plutarch, *Lives*
Polyainos, *Stratagems*
Polybius, *The Histories*
Quintus Curtius, *History of Alexander*
Strabo, *Geography*
Xenophon, *Anabasis*
Xenophon, *Hellenica*
Xenophon, *Kyropaidia*
Xenophon, *On horsemanship*
Xenophon, *The cavalry commander*

Secondary sources
Cernenko, E.V., *The Scythians 700–300 BC* (Osprey Publishing, 1983).
Connolly, P., *Greece and Rome at War* (Frontline Books, 1981).
DeSantis, M.G., 'Old men's war: the Silver Shields after Alexander', *Ancient Warfare Magazine*, volume IX, issue 5.
Evers, R., 'A one-man army: the forces of Epirus', *Ancient Warfare Magazine*, volume VI, issue 4.
Gorelik, K., *Warriors of Eurasia* (Montvert Publishing, 1995).
Head, D., *Armies of the Macedonian and Punic Wars* (Wargames Research Group, 1982).
Heckel, W. and Jones, R., *Macedonian Warrior* (Osprey Publishing, 2006).
Kambouris, M.E., 'The Hypaspist Corps', *Ancient Warfare Magazine*, volume IX, issue 5.
McDonnel-Staff, P., 'Hypaspists to Peltasts: the elite guard infantry of the Antigonid Macedonian Army', *Ancient Warfare Magazine*, volume V, issue 6.
Nikorov, V.P., *The Armies of Bactria 700 BC–450 AD* (Montvert Publishing, 1997).
Post, R., 'Bright colours and uniformity: Hellenistic military costume', *Ancient Warfare Magazine*, volume IV, issue 6.
Sekunda, N., *Macedonian Armies after Alexander 323–168 BC* (Osprey Publishing, 2012).
Sekunda, N., *The Army of Alexander the Great* (Osprey Publishing, 1984).
Taylor, M.J., 'The Macedonian conscription diagramma', *Ancient Warfare Magazine*, volume IX, issue 5.
Webber, C., 'Fighting on all sides: Thracian mercenaries of the Hellenistic Era', *Ancient Warfare Magazine*, volume IV, issue 6.
Webber, C., *The Thracians 700 BC–AD 46* (Osprey Publishing, 2001).

The Re-enactors who Contributed to this Book

Hetairoi e.V.

Hetairoi e.V. is an association of people who have taken interest in various aspects of ancient Greek life and culture. Our goal is to recreate as many aspects as possible of the lives of people in ancient Greece as well as in neighbouring cultures. Our chosen method is called 'Living History', a concept developed out of battle re-enactments. Contrary to re-enactments, Living History interpreters make use of third-person interpretation, where they wear recreated clothing and equipment, but remain available for the audience to answer any questions and explain their activities. Sometimes short historical scenes are re-enacted, usually narrated by a member of the group explaining what is happening to the audience.

From 2018, our members have been able to show reconstructions from the early Classical era, around 500 BC, to the late Hellenistic period, around 100 BC. Because you can't fully understand a culture without studying its neighbours, we have also recreated historical impressions from the important Greek neighbours of Rome, Persia, southern Italy, Thrace and Scythia. It is very important that the reconstructed equipment and clothing are based on the historic originals as closely as possible. We strive to base our recreations on the latest state of scientific research, and invest a lot of time in research before starting our work. If we can't craft the pieces ourselves, our reconstructed equipment is sometimes created by craftsmen, who are specialized in reconstructions for museums.

The Hetairoi are at your service for events in museums or educational institutions, or other events where the transfer of knowledge is the main focus. As such we have among others already collaborated with museums like the Ephesos Museum and the Kunsthistorisches Museum in Vienna, the Reiss-Engelhorn-Museen in Mannheim, the Varusschlacht Museum und Park Kalkriese and the Historisches Museum der Pfalz in Speyer.

Contacts:
E-mail: info@hetairoi.de
Website: http://hetairoi.de
Facebook: https://www.facebook.com/Hetairoi.de

Athenea Prómakhos

Athenea Prómakhos was created in Saragossa, Spain, during 2004, having as its main objective that of recreating and divulging the history and daily life of the ancient Greek warriors. The group was officially registered as a non-profit cultural association in April 2006. In Greek mythology, Athenea (Athena) was the goddess of wisdom, skill and arts. Consequently, together with Apollo, she was the religious entity who represented in the best possible way the national spirit of the ancient Greeks. In addition, Athena was a warrior-goddess, having the term Prómakhos (i.e. warrior) among her most important attributes. Unlike the blind violence and thirst for blood that characterized the fighting style of her brother Mars, Athena's military actions were guided by great intelligence and she usually preferred peaceful solutions to war (at least when possible). As a result of this, the group derives its name from this peculiar faculty of Athena (i.e. Athena the warrior).

With the progression of time, Athenea Prómakhos has grown considerably and now comprises many members living in every corner of Spain. The association has not only expanded numerically, but also in its range of activities. It has greatly augmented the number of topics covered by its activities: after years of research and practical experience, the group is now able to cover all general aspects of the ancient Greeks' daily life. This means that the activities performed by the group are not focused only on military aspects, but also on the civil life of Greek communities. In addition, members of Athenea Prómakhos are now able to reconstruct the daily life of the foreign communities that came in contact with the Greeks, either as allies or as enemies. These had a great influence over the development of Greek civilization and culture across the centuries. All the activities of Athenea Prómakhos are based on accurate research and analysis of all the most important primary sources dating back to the Classical period, be they literary or archaeological. Our research is supplemented by methodical consultation of all the scientific publications dedicated to the history and archaeology of Ancient Greece and by frequent visits to some of the world's most important museums dedicated to Greek civilization. Thanks to all this, the members of the association have been able to develop a direct and evidence-based knowledge of the objects that they recreate. This is constantly enriched by participation in important historical and archaeological conferences, as well as by the frequent contacts that the association has with important historians and archaeologists of the Greek world.

The main objective of Athenea Prómakhos is the use of a true philological approach in all its re-enacting activities, in order to reproduce the materials and objects in the best possible way and to perform activities of the best quality. All this is made without renouncing the original spirit of historical re-enacting, which comprises important social aspects. Thanks to our research and activities, which have experienced great success over the years, we have been able to participate in important and prestigious events in various European countries. Among these we particularly remember Tarraco Viva, Les Grands Jeux Romaines of Nîmes, re-enacting events at Aquileia and the 2,500th anniversary of the Battle of Marathon in Greece. Athenea Prómakhos has also performed at numerous important museums and archaeological sites, such as those of El Efebo in Agde, Saint-Romain-en-Gal, Loupian, Olbia and Ampurias. We are always open to any kind of collaboration aimed at the divulging of historical and archaeological knowledge related to Greek civilization.

Contacts:
E-mail: apromakhos@gmail.com
Website: www.atheneapromakhos.org
Facebook: https://www.facebook.com/groups/799282110120899/

Ancient Thrace

The living history association Ancient Thrace was created in 2015 as a group for historical re-enactment by enthusiasts from Yambol in Bulgaria, who were fascinated by the ancient history of their land and wanted to express their passion for it. By now the association has around twenty regular members and many more friends from different places who often join its activities. The efforts of our group have as their main aim that of reconstructing the lifestyle, culture and military equipment of the Thracian tribes in the period from 400 BC–AD 100. With the progress of time, we also started to reconstruct the lives of other peoples living in the Balkans during Antiquity: Celts (300 BC–AD 100), Germani (AD 100–200) and Goths (AD 300–400). In our activities and reconstructions we try to be as historically accurate as we can. Our equipment is based on countless hours of interpreting ancient documents and archeological evidence; our process of research and experimentation never stops. During recent years we have participated with success at several festivals in Bulgaria and abroad, and have also collaborated in the creation of various movies and books. All these positive experiences have increased our confidence and stimulated the general improvement of our group. Since we created Ancient Thrace, we have visited numerous amazing destinations and met many great people, learned more about history and shared great memories together. For us, historical re-enactment is a special passion that combines our interest with history with our desire to learn more about the past. We wish to reach people and share with them the emotions of this passion, which has become a very important component of all our daily lives.

Contacts:
Facebook: https://www.facebook.com/AncientThrace/

Index